Unspeakable Acts
Unnatural Practices

Books by Frank Smith

Understanding Reading (five editions)

Writing and the Writer (two editions)

Comprehension and Learning

Reading Without Nonsense (three editions)

*Insult to Intelligence**

to think

Whose Language? What Power?

The Book of Learning and Forgetting

The Glass Wall: Why Mathematics Can Seem Difficult

Edited volumes

The Genesis of Language (with George A. Miller)

Psycholinguistics and Reading

Awakening to Literacy (with Hillel Goelman and Antoinette A. Oberg)**

Essays

*Essays Into Literacy**

*Joining the Literacy Club**

*Between Hope and Havoc**

*Unspeakable Acts, Unnatural Practices**

*Published by Heinemann

Unspeakable Acts
Unnatural Practices

FLAWS AND FALLACIES IN
"SCIENTIFIC" READING INSTRUCTION

FRANK SMITH

HEINEMANN
PORTSMOUTH, NH

Heinemann
A division of Reed Elsevier Inc.
361 Hanover Street
Portsmouth, NH 03801–3912
www.heinemann.com

Offices and agents throughout the world

The author and publisher wish to thank those who have generously given permission to reprint borrowed material:

Cover illustration "Big Fish Eat Little Fish" by P. Bruegel courtesy of the Albertina Museum, Wien, Austria.

Chapter 4 is based on the article "Why Systematic Phonics and Phonemic Awareness Instruction Constitutes an Educational Hazard" in *Language Arts* 77, 2. Copyright © 1999 by Frank Smith.

Chapter 5 is based on the article "The Just So Story—Obvious But False" in *Language Arts* 80, 4. Copyright © 2003 by Frank Smith.

Chapter 8 was previously published in *Phi Delta Kappan* 82, 8. Copyright © 2001 by Frank Smith.

Chapter 9 is adapted from *The Glass Wall* by Frank Smith. Copyright © 2002 by Frank Smith. Published by Teachers College Press.

Chapter 10 is based on an article of the same name published in *Language Arts* 76, 2. Copyright © 1999 by Frank Smith.

Library of Congress Cataloging-in-Publication Data
Smith, Frank, 1928–
    Unspeakable acts, unnatural practices : flaws and fallacies in "scientific" reading instruction / Frank Smith.
        p.   cm.
    Includes bibliographical references and indexes.
    ISBN 0–325–00619–9 (pbk. : alk. paper)
    1. Reading.   2. Written communication.   I. Title.
LB1050.S5734   2003
372.4—dc21   2003008738

Editor: Lois Bridges
Production: Lynne Reed
Cover design: Night & Day Design
Typesetter: House of Equations, Inc.
Manufacturing: Steve Bernier

Printed in the United States of America on acid-free paper
07 06 05 04 03 VP 1 2 3 4 5

CONTENTS

PREFACE

The title of this collection of essays should be taken literally. Reading instruction that is claimed to be "scientific," "research-based," and "evidence-based"—imposed on many teachers and enforced through innumerable mandated tests—is founded on activities that are unspeakable and practices that are unnatural.

The instruction to which I refer focuses on early and intensive training in phonics and phonemic awareness. The underlying idea is that by "sounding out" the spelling of a written word an intelligible spoken word will be produced. But the sounds produced by phonic "decoding" only remotely resemble the sounds of spoken language. Comprehensible speech cannot be produced by melding sounds associated with alphabetic characters, either by humans or by computers. The sounds that phonic activities are expected to produce are literally unspeakable.

The instruction to which I refer is also predicated on the idea that children learn complex skills by being taught parts of those skills, which they then somehow integrate into a complete and comprehensible act. But children do not develop meaningful abilities by practicing meaningless activities. Their natural response to something that makes no sense to them is aversion. Expecting them to behave otherwise is indeed unnatural.

A major justification for the pointless activities that children are expected to engage in as a basis for learning to read is that reading itself is an unnatural activity. Learning to talk is supposed to be "natural," almost as if nothing need be done by a child in order for spoken language to appear spontaneously, but learning to make sense of written symbols is somehow against nature, and requires special mental contortions in order to convert meaningless marks to meaningful sounds. The very idea is ludicrous, and will be addressed in the first essay.

Chapter 1 explains why learning to read is natural.

Chapter 2 laments that the marvel of reading is misrepresented as a mystery.

Chapter 3 clarifies terms frequently used in relation to reading, such as *phonics*, *phonemics*, *phonology*, and *phonetics*.

Chapter 4 outlines why instruction in phonics and phonemic awareness can be an educational hazard.

Chapter 5 focuses on the fallacy of "sounding out" unknown words.

Chapter 6 discusses the narrow view of some influential studies commissioned by U.S. federal agencies.

Chapter 7 presents an alternative scenario showing how readers routinely discover the meaning and pronunciation of unfamiliar written words without phonics.

Chapter 8 argues that educational "problems" are often a matter of bad timing.

Chapter 9 examines reading and comprehension difficulties related to mathematics instruction.

Chapter 10 takes a broad view of teaching and technology.

Chapters 4, 5, and 10 are based on articles published in *Language Arts* (Smith 1999b, 2003, 1999a, respectively); Chapter 8 was previously published in *Phi Delta Kappan* (Smith 2001). Part of Chapter 9 is taken from my book on mathematics, *The Glass Wall*, published by Teachers College Press (2002). All other text is new and previously unpublished.

My title is derived, with an appropriate inversion, from an entertaining collection of short stories by Donald Barthelme (1968). His title has stuck in my memory for thirty-five years, which I take to be a good omen. The idea of the present collection came from my constant colleague and editor Mary-Theresa Smith. I also thank her for thinking of Socrates and Bruegel.

CHAPTER ONE

WHY READING IS NATURAL

Proponents of direct, intensive, and early phonics training for teaching reading partly justify their peculiar instructional beliefs by asserting that, unlike learning spoken language, learning to read is not "natural," and that reading itself is an unnatural activity. This book takes a contrary position.

To clear the ground for my arguments, I must deal with several matters that in my view contribute to profound confusions or misconceptions about the nature of reading. They concern (1) the alphabet, (2) language, (3) the brain. I raise these issues now because to some extent they contradict what often seems obvious, and there is no point in making an analysis of reading instruction without first examining critically what many people may take for granted.

THE ALPHABET

Ever since an alphabetic writing system was invented by the Greeks about two thousand years ago, the twenty-six or so letters have had a profound influence on human thought. Many people through the centuries have been fascinated by the letters that make up words, and the putative relationships of these letters to the sounds of speech. They cannot imagine reading without a role for the letters that make up individual words.

Reading instruction from the times of the Greeks and Romans has focused on letters and sounds, despite continual efforts by critics to emphasize the central role of meaning in reading and to demonstrate that letters play only a small, redundant, and usually confusing part. Letters have become a fetish. People transfixed by the alphabet ask incredulously what the purpose of letters might be if not to make it possible for readers to read.

But the alphabet was never designed to help readers. It wasn't invented or developed for that purpose. Nor was it intended to be of particular help to writers. The alphabet's true function has always been to help people cope with technical problems of making language visible on various contrasting surfaces, to scribes, copyists, inscribers, and printers. I'll call them transcribers.

The prime importance of the alphabet is that it enables people to make marks on paper (and other surfaces) in a simple and consistent manner, so that written words will always look the same. In a sense, the twenty-six letters are convenient alternatives to drawings. They are building blocks for the construction of visible words, like the wooden tablets used in many board games. "Decoding to sound" has nothing to do with it. Readers had already been coping with nonalphabetic languages like Chinese for centuries, and continue to do so. Learning to read a pictographic or ideographic script has never been a particularly complicated or traumatic process. Even in alphabetic cultures today we all cope with a multitude of symbols that don't decompose into individual sounds, like the ubiquitous ⊘ ("don't even think about it") signs; the icons on washroom doors, dashboards, and laundry machines; numerical symbols such as 1, 2, 3, and so forth; and such characters as @ # $ % ^ & * ( ) + = ? on keyboards. They may have names, but they can't be broken down into sounds. Nor has the alphabet anything to do with *encoding*, for that matter. Letters reflect sounds in written words only coincidentally; they are guidelines that keep transcribers from selecting letters in an idiosyncratic and arbitrary manner. Letters cut down on arguments. No one can claim that C-O-W is a better way of writing "horse" than

H-O-R-S-E. But this was far more important for the transcriber than the writer. In fact it was not until after the Gutenberg revolution, when texts began to be mass-produced, that printers began to worry particularly about consistency. They didn't want spellings that sounded right, just ones that weren't contentious (to avoid arguing about whether "wagon" should be spelled with one *g* rather than two).

The principal advantages of the alphabet, the reasons it thrives, have nothing to do with reading. First and foremost, the limited set of letters (they could simply be called shapes at this point) can be used to construct written words that might otherwise require hundreds or even thousands of complex pictographic-ideographic symbols. Alphabets are a construction kit for putting words together—much like the set used by a person who constantly changes the billboards for movie theaters or supermarkets (call him a letterman)—assembling one letter at a time from a stock of 26 alternatives. This is an enormous advantage. From just 26 basic shapes, a unique visual representation of every word in the language can be produced. Even speech is more complicated—it requires about 45 different sounds. The letterman doesn't even need to be literate, as he copies one letter at a time from his script. Just think of the economy if every automobile in the world could be constructed from a couple of dozen basic components. And contrast the cost-effectiveness of having 26 basic shapes from which to build words, compared with the complexity of Chinese script, which has to be drawn by an artist for formal purposes. (A standardized alphabetic form of Chinese became imperative with the advent of keyboards for typewriters and computers.)

The second advantage of the alphabet is that each of these shapes, and their variants, has been given a name—ay, bee, sea, etc.—so that the illiterate letterman can be *told* how to construct every word in the language. Instead of "Use a circle, a zigzag, and a right-angle" he can be told to put up an *o*, a *w*, and an *l*.

When a child asks, "How do I write *cat*?" we don't have to say, "There's an open circle at the beginning, then a closed circle with a tail, and finally a . . ." (I can't even think how to describe a *t*). We simply say, "*Cat* is written *c a t*." We can do that for every word in the language. Try that with an ideographic system.

This far from exhausts the utility of the alphabet. The twenty-six letters have been assigned a conventional order, so that every word in the language, including names, can be put into easily sorted, easily searched sequences. Think of the utility of alphabetical order in dictionaries, directories, libraries, and other information storage and retrieval systems. Imagine the organizational chaos if alphabetical order didn't exist. (How could I construct an index for this book?)

So the alphabet earns its keep; it is one of our most useful inventions. But it isn't essential. We could have visible language without it. People can learn to read without a phonetic alphabet without great difficulty (though learning to write may take a little longer for nonalphabetic scripts). None of this has anything to do with sounds. The sounds associated with letters are largely irrelevant and frequently misleading for readers and writers. Here's a quick illustration of that fact. Computer programs that "read" by producing sounds from text that is keyboarded in, and that "write" by transforming speech input into text, never use phonics. The programs won't work at the letter-sound level. And as for "phonemic awareness," the detection of distinct sounds in spoken language that are supposed to correspond to letters, computers can't do it at all. Computers do best with words, especially when grouped in meaningful sequences. Computers aren't lettermen.

LANGUAGE

I don't propose to enter into a lengthy disquisition on the nature of language, or on its uses in society, communication, and expression. I just want to focus on one narrow aspect of language, which has a considerable impact on the way everyone thinks. I want to consider how language *creates* worlds, objects, and relationships, which in no other sense exist. Language makes us think something is there when it isn't. It fools us.

We all know of the credibility of language in fiction, of course. I recently went on a walking tour of Dublin, exploring the Martello tower where Stephen Dedalus lived and eating in the pubs where Leopold Bloom dined. It was only when I left that I realized that I had been following in the footsteps of totally imaginary characters, no more real than Sherlock Holmes or Dr. Who. Imaginary constructs can exist when people think they are real, not fictitious. There was a time when most of the scientific world thought that inflammable materials contained a substance named phlogiston, which caused fires, and that light waves passed through a stuff called ether, which filled up space.

The human race is always prone to give names to aspects of their experience, and then to take for granted that whatever corresponds to those names exists. Give something a name (like intelligence, or perseverance, or wickedness), and many people will think that it exists, not as a kind of behavior that fits a certain description, but as the cause or underpinning of the behavior. Thus reading, for example, which in general is an easily identified behavior, has become transmuted into *the reading process*, which is assumed (by many) to actually exist within the human brain (which is also supposed to contain a writing process, a grammatical process, a phonemic awareness process, and for all I know a sitting-still-on-a-chair process).

Learning and comprehension are particularly interesting examples of this drive to construct fictitious entities. Both are widely regarded as *skills*, reflecting learning and comprehension processes in the brain. Instructional programs are devised to augment these processes, and standardized tests to calibrate their effectiveness. But a different point of view can be taken that learning and comprehension are simply states of the human organism. They are neither skills nor processes, but a condition of being alive. Their presence in human beings does not have to be explained, only their absence, or rather the consequences of their suppression. Any human in a position of being unable to learn is bored. No one would claim that boredom was a process; it is the opposite of learning, an alternative state. Similarly, absence of comprehension is not a lack of skills, nor the shutting down of a process; it is a state, to which we normally give the name of confusion. It might be tempting to consider confusion as a chaotic disorganization of certain structures of the brain, but it is not. It is simply a state that is the opposite of comprehension. I should perhaps note that both boredom and confusion are aversive; they are not natural states to be in. All human beings strive to be in a continuous state of learning and comprehending, just as they continually strive to breathe.

So there are two potential problems with language. It can lead us to believe that things that don't actually exist are real, and then to devise imaginary processes to describe the existence of these unreal things.

I don't want to belittle language in any way; it obviously has many beautiful and useful characteristics. It enables us to think and to create. Language is particularly useful for *description*—a few well-chosen words can give a powerful image of people or objects, and of many associated characteristics (whether or not the person or object actually exists). But language is distinctly lacking in *explanatory* power. Whether we try to explain a person, a group, or an activity like reading, we quickly fall back on fiction and metaphor. Rather than describe the circumstances in which individuals demonstrate literacy, or learn to become literate, we *invent* explanations. We put mechanisms and processes into their heads.

Little of this explanation-through-fantasy would matter if we were to put two little words into our diagnostic and referential statements—the words *as if*. To say the human brain sometimes functions *as if* it were a computer is altogether less misleading than to say that the brain *is* a computer. The statement that some people read *as if* they employ knowledge of letter-sound correspondences is easier to comprehend, and much easier to discuss rationally, than the blunt assertion that people can read because they employ phonic skills.

Language can be used for the careful dissection and analysis of complex human behavior—but not if it is wielded like a blunt instrument.

THE BRAIN

My point about the brain is simply stated. Despite extravagant claims, no one knows how the brain is ultimately related to anything we see or do in the world. Brain research tells us nothing about anything except the brain itself. We may point to various irregularities in the brain to try to account for why things occasionally go wrong, but we can't use the architecture of the brain to explain why anything we do or think goes right, or even why it occurs.

We can take the brain apart and see how all the bits are joined together. We can poke and prod at parts of the living brain and see how a person reacts. We can see what goes wrong when bits are missing. We can take various kinds of pictures of the brain and see how it heats up as people engage in various kinds of activity or as they think about particular things. But none of this *explains* why we have particular kinds of thoughts or sensations. If a blow to a particular part of my brain makes me see stars, or hear a symphony, I have to tell someone of that fact. No neuroscientist can look inside my brain and say, "He's hearing Mahler's Second right now." No neuroscientist can say why I see green, or taste salt, or experience the scent of a rose. Neuroscientists might claim to have produced a complete wiring diagram of the parts of the brain that seem to be involved in anything I do or experience, but they can never say why I have that particular experience. They can't find a map in my head if I claim to know my way around the university, nor can they find why I might decide to walk from one part of campus to another.

The neuroscientist's situation is no different from that of the television technician who can tell you how the various components of your system work together, and can explain why sometimes you don't get sound or a picture, but who has no way of explaining why the various electromagnetic events that take place on the screen should make you laugh, cry, or switch channels.

We'd think it absurd if our technician told us he had detected a sitcom-sensitive area in the television receiver, or that a particular module accounted for the upbeat attitudes of weather reporters, even though a misdirected screwdriver could certainly interfere with both. Yet neuroscientists have no trouble labeling a reading process in the brain. They will draw diagrams of the inside of the brain with arrows and little boxes labeled <input> <output> <phonemic processing> <memory> and even <understanding>. But they can't explain what goes on in those boxes, or the "information" assumed to pass along the routes indicated by the arrows.

No neuroscientist has ever been able to find any of the twenty-six letters of the alphabet in the brain, nor the connections they are supposed to have with particular sounds, though we are assured that such structures exist (though not in people afflicted with "dyslexia"). The alphabet is doubtless a consequence of something in the brain, but not anything that could be regarded as specialized and dedicated for the purpose of producing and making use of letters. The parts of the brain involved in handling letters could very well be the same parts that are involved in identifying birds or cooking omelets. I see no reason why they should not be. The same applies to phonics skills and phonemic awareness. Even if these things have any real existence in the brain (which I doubt), I have encountered no evidence that they would be any different from processes that enable us to listen to jazz or enjoy a movie.

And since there is absolutely no evidence of how any neurological or chemical processes in the brain might produce reading, it makes no sense to say that there are specialized centers or processes in the brain responsible for reading. Obviously there are parts of the brain involved in reading, and a good number of other activities too, but that is no reason to claim that these areas are *for* reading, any more than you can say that one part of an automobile engine is responsible for getting you to the supermarket and another part for driving to the beach.

I have to admit that *brain* used to be one of my favorite words; I held it responsible for almost everything we do. I still regard the brain as an astonishing instrument, far more remarkable than it is often given credit for, but it makes sense much of the time to refer to the whole person rather than to the individual's cranial contents, though it may sound less scientific. Reading, for example, is best regarded as something done by people rather than by brains. To say the brain "looks," "thinks," or "remembers" is about as appropriate as saying that the stomach enjoys a good meal.

READING THE WORLD

I'll start my discussion of reading with a semantic point. Nothing is unnatural in the eyes of infants. Everything they encounter in the world is natural, even if they find it aversive. The arbitrary division of the world into what nature once provided and what people have subsequently done to it is something that has to be learned. Other creatures never make such a distinction. I doubt whether crows have different categories for cars and houses than they do for rocks and trees. Deer are unlikely to think "Here's where nature ends" when they cross from forest glade to cement highway. "Unnatural" is a concept that doesn't exist outside language.

So what is written language? For a child, print is just another facet of the world, not yet comprehended perhaps, but not different from all the complex sights, sounds, smells, tastes, and textures in the environment, not especially mysterious or intimidating.

And what do infants do when they are born into this wholly natural world? They do as they will for the rest of their lives; they try to make sense of it, to discover how it relates to everything else that they know, to understand its relationship to them, its "meaning." Trying to make sense of any facet of the environment, including print, is a natural activity.

How exactly do infants (and adults) strive continually to make sense of everything they encounter in the world? They *read* it. Reading is the most natural activity in the world.

I am not taking liberties with language here. The word *reading* is properly employed for all manner of activities when we endeavor to make sense of circumstances; its original meaning was "interpretation." We read the weather, the state of the tides, people's feelings and intentions, stock market trends, animal tracks, maps, signals, signs, symbols, palms, tea leaves, the law, music, mathematics, minds, body language, between the lines, and above all—a point I must come back to—we read faces. *Reading*, when employed to refer to interpretation of a piece of writing, is just a special use of the term. We have been reading—interpreting experience—constantly since birth (without a special "reading-the-world" center or process in the brain) and we all continue to do so.

What is this basic reading or "making sense" that we all engage in? I don't think it needs to be explained, or even can be explained. It is what we are. Anyone who didn't try continually to make sense of the world could not be considered a functioning human being. Making sense is a matter of interpreting, relating the situation you are in to everything you know already. Not to part of what you know, but everything, since all our knowledge hangs together. Our understanding of the world, all of the world, is coherent, consistent, and immediate. Once you know that a flame burns, you don't have to say to yourself, "That is a flame, therefore it burns." You know that flames burn. Once you can recognize a truck, you don't have to say to yourself, "That is a truck" and consult some inner encyclopedia. Once you can read the written word *dog* you don't have to say to yourself, "That word says *dog*, I must look up what it means." You know what it means.

What do children do when they encounter an actual dog? They don't say, "I recognize that animal with a particular juxtaposition of wet nose, sad eyes, and floppy ears as a certain kind of dog," nor do they say, "There's a dog" to themselves and look up its meaning in a library in the brain. They certainly don't wait to hear the animal bark to decide what it is. Recognition, whether of dogs and cats or written words, is not a matter of breaking something down to its components, but of integrating it into a larger context.

All learning and comprehension is interpretation, understanding an event from its context (or putting the event into a context). All reading of print is interpretation, making sense of print. You don't worry about specific letters or even words when you read, any more than you care particularly about headlights and tires when you identify an automobile.

The best strategy for determining the identity or meaning of an unfamiliar word is to work out what it is from context. As we shall see, this happens very quickly. An equally good way in different circumstances is simply to ask someone what it is. Often we don't have to ask. A very poor strategy is to try to "sound it out."

Some people seem to believe that learning to read is a particularly challenging undertaking—despite the ease with which many children accomplish it, and despite how much children have learned in other contexts.

But no one could catalog all the things a human being, even a young child, has been able to make sense of in the world; it would be an impossible task. We live in an enormously complex and complicated world, but the times when individuals are actually confused, even babies, are remarkably few. Children aren't usually confused by written language—until someone tries to *instruct* them on how to read. When people *help* children to read, by reading to them and with them, there is rarely confusion. It is not reading that many children find difficult, but the instruction.

Most of our learning is unsuspected. Perhaps the most complex learning of all involves the human face. Researcher Daniel McNeill (1998) explains how twenty-two pairs of facial muscles are constantly orchestrated to display at least four thousand different expressions, all produced and understood without any instruction at all. Some basic expressions of emotion—such as fear, anger, surprise, disgust, sadness, and enjoyment—may be instinctive, but the majority are learned early in life. These expressions, involving the entire face from the corners of the mouth to the eyebrows, each element operating individually, communicate not just physical states, but agreement, disagreement, encouragement, puzzlement, disbelief, collusion, threat, challenge—and of course interest and desire. When was anyone taught to interpret all this, to read faces? (Or to "write upon" faces, for that matter.)

It is natural for children, and adults, to strive always to make sense of the world, to interpret what everything must mean. So why should written language be particularly difficult? The answer is that it isn't. Reading print is no more complex than reading faces and other things in the world. Making sense of print can't be more complicated than making sense of speech, which begins much earlier. Written words and spoken words share the same kind of grammar, meanings, and other structures. If we can make sense of all the words of spoken language that we know, we can do the same for written words. The actual numbers involved fade before the vast numbers of faces, places, objects, events, expressions, and relationships that we can make sense of in the world. Memory is hardly a problem. Written words are actually easier to discriminate than speech—we can mishear what someone says, or be unable to recover from a lapse in concentration; in writing we can always check back. Some written words are actually easier to discriminate than the objects they refer to. Subjects in a scientific experiment could identify words flashed on a screen faster than they could identify drawings of the objects the words referred to (such as *house*, *dog*, *flower*, and so forth), even after extensive practice on the limited set of alternative words and pictures that were presented.

There is nothing unnatural about any of this, as I have maintained. Written language is no more opaque or impenetrable than anything else in the world, once we have made sense of it (because we have encountered it in circumstances that make sense to us).

So why do some people have so much trouble learning to read? The first reason might be that they are confronted by reading when it is not the best time for them to learn, just as not everyone learns to play the piano, to swim, or to play chess at the same time. They may be too involved in other things, or trying to recover from some trauma. Learning to read is not necessarily a problem at any age—unless there are years of reading confusion and failure in the past. Which leads to the second reason why some people have so much trouble learning to read. They've been confused. Instead of being helped, they've been handicapped. People can be confused by anything.

Difficulty in learning to read doesn't mean that reading is unnatural.

Allusions to "scientific" studies don't prove a thing. If phonics is an impossible system, even for computers, then any experimental study claiming to show that phonic drills have helped children to read must have been looking at something else. In fact, many studies of phonics and phonemic awareness acknowledge that they *are* looking at something else. Instead of looking at reading as a matter of making sense of text, they look at how well children can put sounds to isolated words, and even nonwords, to confirm that they use the alphabetic code. This is like tying children's feet together to prove they must jump before walking.

References to mythical brain disabilities (diagnosed circularly in relation to perceived reading difficulties) explain nothing. Such phantasms are conjured up in the absence of understanding or coherent theory. And even if there were rare brain malfunctions that make it difficult for a few children and adults to read, that doesn't mean that such individuals should be subjected to regimes of unnatural treatment. Such individuals must still be helped to make sense of print—but it will take more time and patience. Calling them disabled is hardly likely to help.

Reading print is as natural as reading faces. Learning to read should be as natural as any other comprehensible aspect of existence. It is sadly ironic that so many teachers help children to become readers by providing stimulating and supportive environments, only to give the credit to the least important (though often the most prominent) part of the day, the phonics drills.

CHAPTER TWO

MAKING A MYSTERY OUT OF A MARVEL

The cataracts at Niagara Falls are a marvel but they're not a mystery; they're a lot of water falling a great distance. They don't need to be explained to be experienced. The Grand Canyon is also a marvel but not a mystery; it's a long, deep, and winding hole in the ground. What is mysterious is how Niagara Falls and the Grand Canyon came into existence, a problem of explication, not of perception or experience.

Anything humans can do is awe inspiring—walking, talking, reading faces, building supersonic aircraft. That is because each in itself is an amazing talent, and human beings are a marvel to behold. But these marvelous talents aren't mysteries, unless we choose to make them so. They are just things human beings do naturally. Parents aren't challenged by the *mystery* of teaching their children to walk, talk, and read faces, they just have to give them support and a nurturing environment. (And if a child is among those who have physiological difficulties in developing any of these natural abilities, the parent's essential role is not changed. The parent still has to give support and a nurturing environment—only more so.) Reading is a marvel, but not a mystery. It is not a complicated matter, until we try to explain it. Reading is simply a matter of looking at print and making sense of it, no more and no less mysterious than looking at faces and making sense of them, or seeing a darkening sky and interpreting it to mean that storms are on the way. Reading is not rocket science.

THE MARVEL
(BUT NOT THE MYSTERY) OF READING

We think reading is a mystery because of a problem we create for ourselves, by choosing the wrong kind of model for reading. We think reading is something that has to be taught, otherwise it will remain a mystery to the learner. But reading is not the kind of thing we think it is, or are frequently told it is.

Reading is not like chess, or golf, or sailing. There are no special moves to be made, no muscles to be trained, and no technical terms to be learned. You don't need a coach for reading, nor a background team of experts, or exercises. You don't need to read books on the subject.

Reading is also not like history, or geography, or science. There are no facts to be memorized; there's no content to be mastered. You don't need to learn a special language in order to talk to other people who do the same thing, no matter how expert they are at it.

Reading is not a crime. There is no decoding to be done, no secrets to unravel, no clues to be pieced together. You don't have to be a detective to learn to read.

I won't discuss whether reading is like mathematics. There's too much to question about the assumptions behind mathematics instruction. I've summarized a few points in Chapter 9.

So what is reading? What other things *is* it like? I've already said: reading is making sense of print, an everyday aspect of most people's visual world. It is precisely what you (I hope) are doing at the moment. You aren't reading the chapter aloud and listening to what you say. You aren't muttering it silently to yourself. (If you are doing either of those things, you're not doing so in order to make sense of what you're reading—you must have made sense of the print before you uttered it aloud or silently.) You certainly aren't decoding each individual letter to arrive at the sound and meaning of the words.

Reading defies easy definition, simply because it is so much a part of what we normally do, interpreting and making sense of the world. It isn't easy to define and describe breathing, or digestion, or the way your fingernails grow, not because these activities are difficult—they normally take place without attention or awareness—but because any attempt to analyze the detail of what is taking place is totally irrelevant to their occurrence. Children don't breathe, eat, or grow any better because someone belabors them with theory about what is going on, or tries to get them to practice "related" activities before actually getting on with the task at hand.

I'll stick with my initial proposal. Reading is making sense of print, just as seeing is making sense of the visual world and hearing is making sense of sound. No explanation is offered because no useful explanation can be found. We don't know what goes on in the brain when we read any more than we know what goes on in the brain when we listen to music, brush our hair, or play golf. We can describe an experience, but we can't describe what we do in our brain in order to have an experience. Any kind of experience can be a marvel, but the experience is not a mystery. It makes sense to say we feel happy, apprehensive, or joyful, but not to try to explain physiologically what it is that enables us to feel any of those sensations. We don't have to practice feeling joyful.

Why then do so many people try to make a mystery out of reading? One reason is that they are determined to reduce reading to decoding letters to sound (the fascination with the alphabet that I described in Chapter 1). Since reading (making sense of print) doesn't involve decoding letters to sound, any attempt to make it do so is bound to be mysterious. Another reason is that many people want to tell teachers how to teach reading (or to buy materials that are supposed to teach reading), and they can only do this by making a mystery out of reading. To sell snake oil, there has to be a problem it will remedy.

Helping a child to become a reader requires no special materials or techniques, only vastly important and precious qualities of patience, tolerance, empathy, and sensitivity. Children learn to read by reading, provided they are interested in what they read and not confused by it. That's Task 1 for the teacher, to find material that will be interesting and comprehensible for each individual learner. There's nothing mysterious or problematic about that (provided the teacher's time has not been taken up with mindless activities).

Task 2 is to help the child to read. Normally the *author* does this, if the book (or comic or magazine) is engrossing and easy to follow. But sometimes the teacher has to help, especially at the beginning. How does a teacher help a child to read? By reading for the child. First reading *to* the child, then reading *with* the child. There's no mystery here, though the consequence may be something to marvel at.

Task 3 is to get out of the way and let the children get on with the reading, which usually means protecting them against assessments, diagnostics, high-stakes tests, interruptions, and other "educational" digressions. The only real mystery is why all the digressions are felt to be necessary.

AN EDUCATIONAL EPISODE

The debate has been going on for thousands of years.

GLAUCON: I've spent all day listening to the sophists in the marketplace, and my head is spinning. Please help me, O great elucidator of mysteries. Just how does a child learn to read?

SOCRATES: I doubt if my humble reflections will be of any use to you in face of the wisdom you have already imbibed. Enlighten me on what you have been taught.

GLAUCON: The consensus of informed opinion, all founded I'm told on the latest indisputable oracle-based research, is that every moment of every day in every schoolroom has to be dedicated to every child learning exactly the same thing at exactly the same moment. Only in that way will the gods be mollified and permit the divine gift of literacy to be transferred into every child's soul. Every normal and disciplined child, that is.

SOCRATES: And how exactly is that much-desired state to come about?

GLAUCON: There has to be an obedient and dedicated high priest in every schoolroom, to inspire awe and respect in every student in the face of the mysteries. The high priest should appear to be omniscient, ready to make life-changing decisions about every child, with knowledge of every student's accomplishments and misdeeds that even the child doesn't know about. The priest ordains everything a child must and must not do in the course of a school day, and can take away the liberty of any transgressor whose offerings fail to please, or who falls by the wayside. Parents must also be in awe of the power of this personage. They may complain behind the priest's back, but they must blame the child for bringing the priest's displeasure down upon the family. They may mutter if the child has to do extra duties in the evenings or at weekends, as if they (the parents) were being deprived of liberty because of their ungrateful offspring.

SOCRATES: And what is it the supplicants must do in the sanctified precincts of the schoolroom?

GLAUCON: First there are the rituals of going quietly to their appointed place, respectfully taking out the sacred materials, rising when called upon, giving the correct responses to the catechism, sitting quietly while other children are reading aloud, and waiting anxiously to be called upon themselves. Naturally, the most apprehensive students are the sinners who are failing to keep up with the rest. There are also incantations to be solemnly recited: "*guh o duh suh* says *gods, muh eh nuh* says *men.*" Perform these venerable chants, fill in the mystic spaces in the cabalistic lists of words and near words, and the gods will be propitiated. One hopes.

SOCRATES: *Guh o duh suh* doesn't say *gods*. It's positively un-speakable. I'm sure any god who heard such mangled utter-ances would be outraged.

GLAUCON: I'm assured that it works, if you make the sounds quickly enough, often enough, subvocally and automatically. After a lengthy apprenticeship with this kind of exercise, any child can recite decodable Greek.

SOCRATES: Decodable Greek?

GLAUCON: That's a special language that only the gods can understand.

SOCRATES: And if the divine gift of literacy is withheld?

GLAUCON: Naturally the high priest is blamed. Behind every pastoral worker is a superior in the high temple with the power to excommunicate dilatory priests and recalcitrant acolytes, aided by a consistory of experts handpicked not to undermine the infallibility of the official doctrine. It is all reliable, replicable, oracle-based research. If the prescription fails, the high priest or the students must be to blame. It is an indictable offense to criticize the oracle.

SOCRATES: And you believe all this?

GLAUCON: Who am I to challenge such consolidated convic-tion?

SOCRATES: Who indeed? And if you do believe, I have a barely used Doric temple up on the Acropolis that I could get for you cheap.

GLAUCON: You think there is a better way, Socrates?

SOCRATES: It's not up to me to assert such a thing. But I'm sure you already have an alternative in your head. Let's talk about an actual individual rather than about learners as an abstrac-tion. Don't you think it time that the nephew of whom you are so proud read a few books rather than spending all day playing dice with his friends and sticking the prongs of his trident into inoffensive fish?

GLAUCON: Indeed I do, Socrates. But how should I bring this about?

SOCRATES: You are a reasonable man, Glaucon. I have no good advice for you, but I'm sure you can manage without. Assuming you are fortunate enough not to have the vouchers to send your nephew to the academy, how would you go about making him a reader?

GLAUCON: I suppose I'd have to take him down to the marketplace and buy him an interesting book.

SOCRATES: Some inspiring piece of erudition by Sophocles or Euripides, no doubt.

GLAUCON: I would think some of the racier tales of the Trojan wars would be more to his taste.

SOCRATES: So be it. Then you'd take the boy and the book home, shut them both in his chamber, and wait for the learning to occur?

GLAUCON: I don't think that would work, Socrates. I guess I'd begin by reading the book to him myself.

SOCRATES: That sounds like a time-consuming task, especially as you don't have any slaves.

GLAUCON: I wouldn't have to do it all myself. There are lots of people who are always dropping in. I'd get them to read to the boy. They might also bring him a book or two themselves. He's always interested in what motivates other people, especially if it looks a bit illicit.

SOCRATES: You aren't afraid he'd become dependent on other people reading to him?

GLAUCON: You don't know my nephew. The moment he thinks he can do something for himself he won't let anyone else come near him. He'd snatch the book out of my hand—and kick my shins into the bargain.

SOCRATES: But supposing your plan doesn't work? Would you devise some suitable punishment to keep him at his reading?

GLAUCON: What a waste of time that would be. It would defeat the entire purpose of the enterprise. If I can't interest him in reading this week, I'd wait till next week, or next year. There are lots of other useful things that he could learn.

SOCRATES: Well, Glaucon my friend, it looks as if you've done it again. I can always rely on you to generate some good common sense when you put your mind to it. I think you should go back to all those sophists who confused you so much, and show them that you have a much better idea.

GLAUCON: They'd laugh at me, Socrates. They'd ask for my validated, replicated, oracle-based evidence, and vilify me as a heretic. They'd pelt me with rotten tomatoes.

SOCRATES: I can understand your wanting to avoid that, Glaucon. So what do you think you might do if you were responsible for your nephew's education?

GLAUCON: At the very least I would protect my nephew and myself by trying not to draw the wrath of the educational militia down upon us. And maybe I could find some others who share the same point of view, so that we could present a united front to the authorities.

SOCRATES: That all sounds most reasonable to me, Glaucon. I'm impressed that you could come up with all these ideas yourself.

GLAUCON: I can't help suspecting that some of the credit should go to you, Socrates. My friends and I always seem to get better ideas when you listen to us so patiently. We've been thinking perhaps we could nominate you for one of those civic commissions on education that are always being appointed. Short hours, good pay, lots of prestige, and you automatically become a member of the academic elite. But now I have the feeling you wouldn't be interested.

SOCRATES: Another amazing insight, my friend. I think I'd rather drink hemlock.

CHAPTER THREE

CLARIFYING SOME PHON-EY WORDS

It may be helpful to review briefly a few specialized terms, used widely and often indiscriminately by reading theorists and researchers: *phones, phonology, phonetics, phonemes, phonemics,* and *phonics.*

The natural sounds of speech are as turbulent and intermingled as the waters of a rushing stream. Nevertheless, linguists and other scientists attempt to isolate basic elements of spoken language. The smallest unit they can detect is called a *phone,* which is not anything that anyone can normally distinguish or reproduce. Phones are like atoms; they have no real existence in isolation and are modeled more by diagrams than actual replicas. The specialized study of phones and their production is called *phonology* or *phonetics,* the concern of *phonologists* or *phoneticians*—pairs of terms that are largely synonymous.

Phonologists and phoneticians are linguistics specialists concerned with the complex physiology of speech production and perception, the way in which nerves, muscles, the breath, the vocal cords, tongue, teeth, lips, and oral and nasal cavities are orchestrated to produce the sounds of speech. Speakers aren't normally aware of all this background activity, and being told about it doesn't help them to speak differently (though that doesn't prevent some experts from trying to teach phonology to students, especially those whose first language isn't English, in the hope that it will improve their pronunciation).

Phonemes are perceptual rather than physical phenomena, abstract composites of phones. They are defined as the smallest units of sound that differentiate one spoken word from another. Thus the initial sounds of *tip* and *dip* are phonemes, and so are the final sounds of *see* and *saw*. The /t/ phone at the beginning of *tip* is not the same as the /t/ phone at the beginning of *top* (the following sound makes a difference to both of them) but since these two different /t/ phones do not differentiate one word from another—perceptually they are the same—they are not regarded as different phonemes. The study of phonemes is called *phonemics*. The number of phones in most languages exceeds 100, but the number of phonemes is much fewer—about forty-five in English, depending on the analyzer and the dialect. Neither phones nor phonemes exist in written language, nor do they correspond directly to the letters of alphabetic written languages. To refer, as I have, to a phone or phoneme as /t/ is conventional but may be misleading. The *sound* represented by the symbol /t/ is a product of the vocal system; it is not a letter and should not be confused with one. Phonologists and phoneticians use an extended cast of characters to denote sounds, such as ɞ, ɖ, and ʓ, which at least do not look as if they have anything to do with reading.

Phonemic awareness is supposed to be a learned or teachable ability of children to detect the phonemic structure of spoken words. In one sense all children who have learned to talk must have this ability, so that they can produce and understand the sounds of speech themselves. On the other hand, the ability to *say* what the phonemes are in spoken words is not something of any importance in producing or understanding speech (any more than you need to be able to say what you are doing with your muscles in order to walk). Nor is phonemic awareness a necessary part of learning to read. Phonemic awareness is only relevant to a particular kind of reading instruction called *phonics* (see below), and it is usually only people who can read who can make any sense of discussions about phonemic awareness.

23

Graphemes have nothing to do with speech but are characters in writing systems, like the letters of the alphabet. *Phonics* is concerned with connections (or *correspondences*) between phonemes and graphemes. Phonics is not a scientific study at all, but a method of instruction, specifically concerned with teaching children relationships between graphemes and phonemes (or between letters and sounds), the limited utility of which is discussed in Chapters 4 and 5. Phonics is sometimes incorrectly referred to as "phonetics," just as phonemic awareness may also be called "phonological awareness." It can all be very confusing.

Incidentally, neither phonology nor phonemics refers to the way spoken language actually sounds. Even phones are complex productions. The voice is not like a flute, playing one distinct note at a time. It isn't even like a piano, producing chords. If an instrumental analogy has to be found, it would have to be an entire orchestra, with all the different parts of the vocal apparatus making their unique contributions at a slightly different time from the others. To synchronize their contributions, for example, the vocal cords have to be activated earlier than the tongue or lips. Human conductors can't draw notes from instruments in different places on the stage so that their component sounds arrive at the audience's ears at exactly the same moment.

Finally it might also have been noted that I offer no definition of the word *reading*. That is because unlike all the "*phon-*" words, *reading* is not a specialized term with a narrow range of meaning. Every literate person knows what the word reading means when it is used in an everyday context; the people who create difficulties are those who want to use the word in narrow and contentious ways. Reading need not involve any of the *phon-ey* words, except to the extent that they are imposed upon teachers and learners from outside.

As I pointed out in Chapter 1, the word *reading* can be used in a wide variety of contexts, usually without any confusion, to mean something like "to interpret" or "to make sense of." That is the kind of meaning I have in mind when I talk about reading print or reading text. I don't take reading to mean "decoding to sound," or anything else that tries to tie written language directly to the sounds that are produced in speech.

I have also not thought it necessary to define "learning to read," even though some people believe this is an actual and observable "process." We can see that children have learned more about reading when they demonstrate that they read more than they could in the past, a consequence of gaining more reading experience. But we can't catch them in the act of learning to read. There is no "learning to read" process, any more than there is a "growing tall" process. We never say "Johnny's in the next room, growing," though we might observe that he has grown a lot in the past couple of months. We don't need to say, "Johnny's upstairs learning to read." Growth is not something you can observe as a process, though you can certainly see whether someone has grown or not. Learning to read, like physical growth, is a natural occurrence, not a process but a condition.

CHAPTER FOUR

HOW PHONICS CAN BECOME AN EDUCATIONAL HAZARD

There is intense and growing pressure for the universal adoption of systematic phonics and phonemic awareness instruction as the sole method of teaching reading. Duress has reached the point where the U.S. federal government and a number of other administrations have actually begun to legislate how teachers should teach reading and other subjects.

I shall make the following points:

- Systematic phonics is destined to fail as a method of teaching reading, and will make learning to read more difficult for many children.

- The methodology totally misunderstands or ignores how children actually learn to read.

- The time to learn phonics, if at all, is during reading.

- Phonemic awareness is a spurious concept.

- The highly touted "reliable, replicable, scientific research" promoting systematic phonics and phonemic awareness instruction is narrow, unrealistic, and tendentious.

- Systematic phonics and phonemic awareness instruction is the thin end of a wedge to bring about radical changes in education, primarily driven by commercial and ideological agendas.

THE ISSUES

The question of how reading should be taught is currently couched in terms of phonics vs. whole language instruction. The focus on whole language is largely a red herring and strategic ploy, used—or misused—by some proponents of phonics to advance their tenuous cause. But the underlying issues are much more general, concerning the nature of reading, learning, and teaching.

The issue concerning the nature of reading is whether reading is a matter of constructing meaning or decoding to sound. The issue concerning learning is whether the learner should play an active or passive role in learning to read. The issue concerning instruction is whether teachers or outside experts and authorities should be in charge of classrooms.

Each of these issues would take a book to discuss in detail. In fact I have written at least one book on each: Smith (1994, 1997) on reading; Smith (1998) on learning, and Smith (1986) on instruction. In the following paragraphs I present only brief commentaries on each of the three issues. Then I examine phonics.

The Nature of Reading

Human beings are adept at making sense of the world around them through all their senses. We use our ears to pick up sounds that we usually identify immediately. We try to make every noise meaningful, without converting it into speech. If I hear a bird singing, I don't have to tell myself I hear a bird singing before I understand what is going on. If I hear a floorboard creak during the night, I don't have to run through a list of verbal possibilities before I can imagine what the cause of the sound might be; my perceptions and imagination always run far ahead of anything I might subsequently say about them. When I hear spoken language, my perception is also direct. I don't have to tell myself what someone is saying in order to understand what is being said. My understanding is direct and unmediated.

The same applies to vision. I don't have to say that I am looking at a cloud in order to understand that I am looking at a cloud, nor do I have to tell myself I am facing an angry dog before I can work out that an angry dog is facing me. There are innumerable visual signs and symbols that I also respond to directly. I don't have to say to myself that a traffic light is red before observing that it is red (and behaving appropriately), nor do I need to announce, "These objects must be a knife and fork" before I know what to do with them. I don't have to say that a sign says "No left turn" before I know what it means. My brain makes sense of the world I encounter with my eyes just as it does with the experiences of my ears or with any of my senses. I don't have to put these experiences into words in order to identify and understand them. The identification and understanding have to be part of my experience before I can talk about them.

It is the same with reading. We don't have to identify individual words before we can work out what they are. We don't have to tell ourselves, "This word is *house*"—converting the written word into spoken language—before we can understand what the written word is. The recognition of meaning is direct: if we have to divert through spoken language we are in trouble. We have no more need to identify and classify individual letters to understand written words than we need to identify and classify individual eyes, noses, and mouths before we can recognize faces.

We often can't pronounce what a written word is until we have identified its meaning. A very familiar example is the word *read*. It is not possible to say whether it should be pronounced "reed" or "red" unless its meaning has been determined from the context it is in: "Would you like to read the book I read yesterday?" The appearance of a written word conveys its meaning directly. That is why we know whether a particular word should be spelled *their* or *there*, or *so*, *sow*, or *sew*. Converting these words to speech would not clarify their meaning, which is implicit in the spelling.

Reading is not decoding to sound. Reading aloud requires comprehension prior to the production of sound. The whole purpose of reading is to make sense of written language, and sense is made of written language directly, not by converting it into sound. As I'll show, it's impossible to convert written words into spoken language with any kind of phonics code. We have to read and understand first and then convert to sound, if that's the intention.

The Nature of Learning

Learning goes on all the time, without our awareness. We learn what makes sense to us (whether the learning is ultimately useful to us or not—we can learn that we can't learn something). We learn what we comprehend. A moment of comprehension is a moment of learning.

Learning has to be meaningful. We don't learn by memorizing whole sets of meaningless pieces that we subsequently put together into a meaningful whole. We learn by being helped to do what we would like to do, or to understand what we are interested in understanding.

Children don't learn to ride a bicycle by first learning the names of all the separate parts. And they don't learn to read by first memorizing a mass of facts about spoken language, or even about superficial aspects of written language, like the alphabet. They learn to read by reading (and if they can't yet read anything for themselves, someone else has to read with them or to them).

The Nature of Teaching

Teaching is a social activity. Predesigned programs can't take the place of teachers, even when the programs are administered by teachers.

Teaching involves decisions made on the spot, not decisions to move from one instructional goal to the next, but decisions related to the condition of the learner. Such conditions might include the learner's (and also the teacher's) physical, emotional, and psychological state at that particular time, together with interest, comprehension, past experience, self-image, feelings about the task at hand, and feelings about the teacher (or about the student).

All these considerations require teachers to interact with and be responsive to learners *personally*, as individuals, not as items on an instructional chart or data on an achievement record.

Conditions for teaching and learning can rarely be perfect, but that doesn't matter if the considerations critical for learning can be addressed by a teacher on the spot, not left to a remote "expert," curriculum designer, or legislator.

THE PROBLEMS WITH PHONICS

The Deceptiveness of Phonics

Superficially, phonics looks as if it should work. Written words are made up of a mere 26 letters and spoken words are made up of about 40 sounds, so why not teach beginners the "spelling-sound correspondences" between letters and sounds so that they can "decode" from written symbols into speech, which is instantly comprehensible?

But written language is not a code for speech; it is an *independent* representation of language. Many written languages are perfectly readable without being alphabetic. We can all recognize and understand symbols that have no alphabetic relation to spoken language, ranging from the icons on computer screens and rest room doors to the numerals and operators of mathematics. Written language doesn't decode to speech in any dependable way, and the number of rules involved in trying to connect letters and sounds is both vast and unreliable. Anyone who tries to read phonetically is a disabled reader. Unfortunately, systematic phonics instruction encourages and even coerces children to try to read phonetically. Teachers who claim they teach intensive phonics with success are directing their credit to the wrong place; they must be doing something else that is right (like helping children to read).

The system of spelling-sound correspondences is so impractical that it is not even used on computers programmed to convert written language into speech. Computers must be programmed to identify whole words, and even then take into account complex grammatical and semantic constraints on how written words should be pronounced. There are many pocket electronic dictionaries and thesauruses with speaking capacity, but they need to have whole words in their data bank; not one of them can produce the sounds of a spoken word through letter-by-letter analysis of spelling.

Even a small vocabulary of 6,000 common words requires over 200 rules to account for all the ways that individual letters are related to individual sounds, and even then the probability of correctly producing the actual sounds of a four-letter word is barely one in four. This research—all scientific, reliable, and replicable, and reported in detail since 1971 in five editions of Smith (1994)—has never been controverted, only ignored by proponents of phonics, presumably because it is unanswerable.

Everyone is familiar with the anomalies of English spelling, from thousands of common words like *so*, *sew*, and *sow*, and *tough*, *bough*, and *through*, to entire poems composed of spelling irregularities. Unpredictability is not the exception in English spelling-sound correspondences, it is the rule.

Being required to master phonics before one can read is the wrong intervention at the wrong time. But ironically, after familiarity with reading is attained, phonics looks deceptively easy and useful. Once you can read a word, you can say which phonics rules apply (for example, that the paired vowels *ea* in *read* should be pronounced one way when the word is in the present tense and another way when it is in the past).

Systematic Phonics and Learning to Read

In itself, phonics is neither good nor bad. It is knowledge, normally acquired unconsciously in the course of reading, the way a multiplicity of details is learned in everyday travels through a familiar landscape. Phonics becomes problematic when it is regarded as an instructional necessity, and a hazard when it is imposed blindly and mindlessly—systematically, in other words—on children who are not yet readers. It becomes a hazard when it takes the place of reading, and especially when it becomes a prerequisite for reading—when students are not enabled to engage in reading until they have fulfilled the requirements of a phonics program. And by then they may have a totally false idea of what reading is really about, and of their own ability to become readers.

Systematic phonics entails nonsensical activities that proceed inexorably from step to step (or rather, from test to test). These activities are boring and discouraging to children, especially to those having difficulty with them, no matter how much they are promoted and dressed up as educational "fun!" (a sure sign that the activity has no redeeming educational purpose). To be drilled in all the contingent relationships between sounds of speech and letters of written language *before children are readers* is a meaningless activity. And once they are readers, *if* they become readers, it is unnecessary.

Phonics is not a system that helps anyone to read, and it can only confuse and interfere with anyone learning to read. That you learn to read by reading has been said so often by so many people that it has become a cliché in literacy education. Yet it doesn't pierce the cognitive blinders of phonics enthusiasts. The most effective literacy teacher is the author of the book a child is enjoying reading, with help if necessary (Meek 1988). For a story that is familiar or predictable, authors show young readers how to recognize and understand every written word. Significant clues to new words, including their pronunciation, come from words that are known already. They, not phonics generalizations, are the most reliable templates for how new words should be understood and pronounced. New words are identified by their visual and meaningful similarities to known words. The more you read, the more you learn about reading, vocabulary, grammar, spelling, and writing (Krashen 1993).

Words in meaningful sequences are the most important elements in reading, not letters or sounds. Words are the smallest independent meaningful units of written language—and even they gain most of their meaning from larger units they are embedded in, such as phrases and sentences. Letters are the construction blocks of written words—the bricks out of which rich and meaningful sequences of words are created. A letter by itself makes no more sense than a brick.

To learn to read you must become familiar with written words, not as imperfect representations of sounds but as significant elements of meaningful language. The best time to do this is while reading, when new words that are encountered are most likely to be meaningful, not from preselected lists of unknown and decontextualized words. This is how infants learn to talk, and how we all expand our vocabularies through life, by encountering new words in meaningful contexts.

It is the same with spelling. We learn correct spellings one word at a time, not from isolated words, or even from "families" of words arbitrarily selected and organized on lists, but from words encountered in reading. Phonics is no help at all. But reading constantly demonstrates not only how words look, but also the complex ways in which their construction is related to meaning, to grammar, and to sound.

Proponents of systematic phonics require all manner of arbitrary and artificial devices to buttress their unnatural practices. Exercises involve meaningless sequences of words—nan can fan dan—and even nonexistent words—gan han lan zan. Words and sentences have blanks in them. Reading materials must be "predictable" or "decodable," which means conforming to phonics generalizations rather than to meaningful language. And "invented" (or creative) spelling is prohibited. Yet we all invent spelling—when we need to write a word whose spelling we don't know and can't look up at the moment. Every spelling mistake that is made (and we all make them) is an invented spelling. The only reason children may exhibit more invented spellings (if they're permitted to) than adults is that they have less experience with how words are conventionally spelled.

Phonics enthusiasts have even invented a spurious physiological or cognitive condition—a lack of something called "phonemic awareness."

Phonemic Awareness

Phonemic awareness (sometimes called phonological awareness) is supposed to be the ability to discriminate individual sounds in spoken words, like detecting that *cat* is made up of the separate sounds /k/ /a/ /t/ (which it isn't; the supposedly discrete sounds are inextricably fused). You can no more separate the sounds from a word that has been uttered than you can extract the ingredients from a cake that has been baked. You can no more blend the sounds of /k/ /a/ /t/ into a single word than you can make a bucket from three bricks. The combination of the separate sounds is unspeakable.

Lack of phonemic awareness is a bogus construct, employed solely to explain the frequent failures of phonics instruction. Instead of questioning the value of systematic phonics, a reason is found for why children might not be profiting from it. When children become confused by the many and varied correspondences between letters of the alphabet and the component sounds of spoken words, it is proposed that the cause is a defective ability to discriminate the sounds of speech. The children are supposed to lack phonemic awareness.

But it's just not true that some children may lack phonemic awareness. Even infants demonstrate an exquisite sensitivity to the phonemic structures of speech. They don't confuse words that have a close similarity of sound, like *pat* and *bat*, or *sip* and *tip*, either in hearing someone else say them or in saying them themselves. (Young children may have articulatory problems in producing some sounds, but that has nothing to do with either phonemic awareness or reading.) No one, except a professional linguist, pays attention to the individual sounds of spoken words; not even proponents of phonics do this. Not being able to say what the component sounds of words are is not the same as being insensitive to them. (We can all distinguish one face from another, but we would be confounded by anyone who asked us how we do it, or required us to talk of the distinguishing features of eyes, noses, and mouths.)

Phonemic awareness is claimed to correlate with reading potential or ability. Of course it does. Children who can read are able to relate the self-evident letters of a spelling—*c-a-t*—with the supposed sounds of a spoken word (especially as teachers often distort the sounds of spoken words during instruction to make them more compatible with spellings). But children forced to pay attention to the nonexistent sounds before they are confident readers are simply bewildered by the instruction.

The current vogue of blaming reading problems on phonemic awareness is reminiscent of the alarm caused in the 1970s by a concept of "cognitive confusion." Some researchers characterized children who had difficulty learning to read who also did not understand such terms a *sentence* and *word* as lacking "cognitive clarity" (Downing and Oliver 1973–74; Downing and Leong 1982). But only *readers* can have concepts of words and sentences. Words and sentences only exist, in any conspicuous form, in written language. Cognitive confusion, like phonemic awareness, had nothing to do with reading, and everything to do with understanding specialized and unnecessary instruction. Once children could read, cognitive confusion disappeared.

The Research Issue

Proponents of systematic phonics make a great deal out of their claim that their assertions are based on reliable, replicable, scientific research studies. So do participants in many fields of endeavor, especially where professional or commercial considerations are at stake.

It is not difficult to devise an experiment that proves a point you want to make, and it is not difficult to ignore research that points in different directions. It is not difficult to claim that favorable research is rigorous and scientific and that other research is unreliable and invalid. Legislation to repudiate research and to punish researchers supporting a particular point of view has not been seen on such a wide scale in the West since the Spanish inquisition.

A typical experimental paradigm begins with a hunch—or a hope—that is treated as the hypothesis being tested. One treatment is contrasted with another, which is supposed to reflect (in the experimenter's mind) an alternative point of view or possibility. Results are rarely clearcut, and differences are often minimal. Research is often designed and conclusions stated less to reveal than to persuade.

Educational studies are especially problematic. They are hard to control unless performed in totally unnatural conditions (which many experimental studies are, to the extent of requiring learners to attempt to identify isolated and intermittent letters or words on a computer monitor while their heads are clamped into a frame). It is almost impossible to segregate experimental subjects into clearly defined groups (children who have received no phonics instruction compared with children who have received only phonics instruction) and it is almost impossible to ensure that the children in the groups receive only the appropriate experimental treatment (the phonics group does no real reading and the others have no insights about phonics).

Taylor (1999) notes that much of the research into the effectiveness of phonemic analysis training uses decoding letter sequences to sound as a measure of achievement, testing what has been taught. She also criticizes the blatant simplification of research design and statistical analyses in studies claimed to have profound implications for education.

There is an alternative. It might be called reflective observation. One advantage of observation, of trying to make sense of particular states of affairs in realistic circumstances, is that the people who are the focus of the study can be treated as individuals. Research that looks for general laws squeezes or stretches everyone to fit into Procrustean beds, and finishes up labeling particular individuals as divergent or handicapped. Experimental research wants to treat everyone as the same; educational practice should always regard everyone as individuals.

Ideological and Commercial Overtones

The campaign to make systematic phonics and phonemic awareness instruction compulsory in all schools has more than an immediate pedagogical threat. The underlying target may not be reading, but education in general. A number of observers (see, for example, articles collected in Goodman 1998a) fear we are seeing just the first overt moves in a campaign to privatize public education and hand it all over to commercial and ideological control.

Producers of systematic educational materials in print and computer software stand to make many millions of dollars in an educational market already worth $1.5 billion a year. Several well-known researchers who advocate phonics instruction are also authors or consultants on phonics instructional programs, and the lobbying for legislative change has been heavily supported by some major publishing groups, whose materials many schools and teachers have been required to use (Goodman 1998b).

Anything that mandates specific courses of behavior for teachers—even if it were relatively enlightened—constitutes a threat to education. People who care professionally about reading do not normally attempt to assert their views through legislation and litigation. On the other hand, people whose aim is to transform schools into more technological and commercial enterprises are likely to pick reading as a particularly soft and profitable target. Passions are easily swayed, simplistic solutions seem realistic, and teachers can be demonized and deprofessionalized.

What About Whole Language?

I have made no effort to promote or defend whole language in this chapter although whole language is often presented as the only alternative to systematic phonics instruction.

Whole language is widely misunderstood, even among its supporters, and often misrepresented by the people who attack it. It is not an instructional method, and it is not therefore an alternative to systematic phonics. Nor are people who support whole language necessarily "against phonics"—although they may vehemently oppose the manner in which systematic phonics instruction is supposed to be delivered to students.

In other words, whole language is not an alternative to phonics instruction, let alone the only one. Any attempt to set up whole language as a failed or defective system that phonics can rise above is nothing more than a tactical ploy.

Whole language—as I see it—is a philosophy of education that was independently conceived, developed, and spread by large numbers of teachers in many countries who were concerned about the artificial fragmentation of both language and instruction. There are still hundreds of independent TAWL (Teachers Applying Whole Language) groups throughout the English-speaking world. But it is easier to attack a few individuals than a mass movement.

What's Wrong With a "Balanced" Approach?

Proponents of phonics often admit that reading experience is essential if children are to learn to read (or even to make sense of reading instruction). They do not agree that the reading experience is the central part of learning to read, but they acknowledge, tacitly at least, that phonics alone will not make a reader.

Apologists for phonics and other fence-sitters sometimes argue for a combination of methods, or even for "the best of both approaches" as if such a concoction were possible. But it would be like serving a slightly diluted poison with a heavily diluted antidote.

The whole point about systematic phonics instruction is that given too soon it confuses and given too late it is unnecessary. No child or adult learner needs to be subjected to anything more than the benign provision of specific information about phonics when it helps them personally with a specific problem, and only to the extent that it helps them at the time, giving them assistance, not instruction.

The issue is not all phonics or no phonics, or even some phonics now and some phonics later. The issue is: Who's in charge? If teachers break the law if they presume to know more about the students they are teaching than the lawmakers and the lobbyists, how can they claim to be professionals?

When teachers are in control, they can use their initiative and introduce some phonics if their past and present experience tells them it will be helpful to students at the time. Mandated commercial systematic programming doesn't permit teachers to learn from past experience or to capitalize on current insights. They are locked into the instructional delivery system as much as their students are, and when things go wrong, as they almost inevitably will, teachers and students alike get the blame.

If Not Phonics, What?

One reason the phonics offensive has been so effective is that many people have become persuaded that in order to teach reading you must have a method, a set of sequenced materials and activities. The unwarranted attacks on whole language naturally follow because perceived alternatives to phonics must be eliminated.

But children do not become readers because of methodologies. A systematic "whole language" instructional program (a multiple oxymoron), if such a thing existed, would be just as much an educational hazard as systematic phonics.

Children learn to read when *conditions* are right. These conditions include their relationships with books and other reading materials, and their relationships with people who will help them to read. The conditions also include their own unique personalities, their self-image, mood, interest, expectations, and comprehension.

None of the responsibilities for ensuring the appropriate conditions for learning to read can be met by experts or authorities outside the classroom. The conditions can't be prepackaged in commercialized kits of learning materials, electronic or otherwise. And the conditions certainly can't be mandated by any kind of legislation. The only person authorized to make all these responsible decisions should be a competent teacher.

CHAPTER FIVE

THE JUST SO STORY— OBVIOUS BUT FALSE

It's obvious, isn't it? You just sound out letters, and you read. C-A-T spells *cat*, right?

That is what my neighbors say when the topic of teaching reading comes up. It's what newspaper columnists, politicians, and publishers of educational tests and instructional materials seem to believe. And it's what large numbers of self-professed experts want every teacher to believe.

I call it the Just So story—Just S-O—Just Sound Out, and you can read.

But the Just So story is false. This isn't just my opinion; it *has* to be false, logically and linguistically. Many teachers know that it's false, though they're not allowed to act on that knowledge. Sometimes they can be sanctioned for even talking about it.

Just So may seem obvious, just as it is obvious that the earth is flat, the sun travels round the earth, and flying machines will take off only if they flap their wings like birds. Obvious, but false.

The belief can only be undermined by deep and critical thought, which is not evident in most casual conversations, media discussions, political pronouncements, and educational planning. People whose mind is already made up don't need to think about something that is obvious.

My neighbors have other things on their minds, and rarely hear an opposing point of view. Challenges to unconsidered beliefs may provoke emotional reactions ranging from defensiveness to hostility, even among friends.

Journalists, politicians, and educational experts and administrators may have a lot more at stake, including their jobs. Entire theories of teaching reading are based on the Just So story. How do you persuade people it is false when it is not in their interest even to think about the possibility?

They must be shown that (1) sounding out is a handicap, not a help, to reading, and (2) there is a better alternative.

SOUNDING OUT IS A HANDICAP

The primary reason why sounding out doesn't help anyone is that it is unreliable. There are too many alternatives and exceptions. Every letter of English can represent more than one sound (or silence), and every sound of English (including silence) can be represented by more than one letter. There are over 300 ways in which letters and sounds can be related. These are the "rules of phonics" that sounding out advocates expect children to learn in order to "decode" written words into sound.

C-A-T is not necessarily *k-a-t*. We only think C-A-T is *cat* because we know how the word *cat* is spelled. Therefore it's obvious. *C* can also be *s* (*c*ity), *a* can be *uh* (*a*bout) and *t* can be *ch* (pic*t*ure)—so C-A-T could equally well spell *such*.

Everybody knows words that are "spelled irregularly." They include most of the words in the English language. Entire poems have been written highlighting such words. It would be difficult to write a poem using words that *aren't* exceptions.

This isn't a matter of picking exceptions to show that sounding out is unworkable. On the contrary, exceptions (like *c-a-t*) must be selected to try to show that sounding out works. In the trade it's called *decodable text*. Try reading some; it's not real English.

The probability is that you'll make at least one mistake in reading *any* (annie?) English word if you rely on sounding out letters. That's why computer programs that "read" English text aloud do so by recognizing entire words (or syllables by default) rather than individual letters. Reading by sounding out is impossible. Sounding out is the ultimate unspeakable act.

The brain has no time to decode letters to sound when you read, and even less when you are trying to learn to read. And the purpose of reading is not to produce sounds of words, but to understand their meaning. Readers must understand what they are reading before they can read aloud. Try reading aloud a language you don't understand.

Incidentally, sounding out doesn't help you spell. Peepul hoo rite werds the weigh thay sownd ar the werst spelerz.

It is frequently asserted that phonics must be right because it is "based on research." No research has ever demonstrated that children can learn to read solely by being taught to sound out—that would be cruel and unnatural treatment—though millions have learned without recourse to sounding out at all. The effect of phonics instruction is often tested on real or made-up "words" that are easily sounded out, which is no test at all.

THERE IS A BETTER ALTERNATIVE

Readers can't read just by decoding letters to sound, and children don't learn to read in that way. They read by recognizing words.

Learning to recognize thousands of words on sight is not a problem. We can all recognize thousands of different faces and objects. It is easier to learn to distinguish printed words than it is to distinguish faces and objects.

Most people read languages that have no letters. It doesn't take Chinese speakers any longer to learn to read their non-alphabetic languages than it does for English speakers to learn to read English. Hearing-impaired children learn to read.

Many English-speaking children learn to read before they are exposed to sounding out, and most children only understand sounding out once they can read. Reading doesn't usually confuse children, even when they are learning. Sounding out is so confusing that its proponents have had to invent a new physical disability to explain why so many children don't understand it.

Children who have difficulty with sounding out are said to lack the ability to hear the sounds of spoken words properly. But oddly enough, that doesn't prevent such children from understanding spoken words. They don't hear the word *cat* as "such." Lack of "phonemic awareness" is a handicap that only strikes children who can't make sense of the instruction, and it is cured by learning to read.

So why are there letters of the alphabet? It's a long story, which has nothing to do with readers or writers. Letters were devised to make life easier for scribes and printers, so they could break written words down into replicable units. Today they facilitate the use of keyboards. Letters are an easy way of talking about words; they help us organize directories and lists. It's an historical accident that we've got them. Relating letters to the sounds of speech has nothing to do with reading or writing.

We can read because we become familiar with the shapes of words, we can recognize them; and we can write because we become familiar with spellings, we can remember them (not always correctly, of course, but sounding out won't cure that).

This doesn't mean that the best way to learn to read and write is by studying lists of words. That would be as foolish as listing in advance the words an infant is to be taught every day when learning to talk. Words are not learned by rote, one at a time, when they are as meaningless as letters. They are learned when they make sense.

Children learn to recognize written words in stories that are interesting and comprehensible to them. At the beginning they need someone to read to them, or with them, but very soon the act of reading itself makes new words familiar and recognizable. Every word learned is a convenient package of clues for recognizing other words. Some children even succeed in learning to read without adult assistance, helped no doubt by the pictures that accompany interesting stories and other texts.

But whether children learn quickly or slowly, with minimal assistance or with considerable labor, it is only by reading that they learn to read. They have to become familiar with the look of written words, not with their sounds.

So why is a fallacious story so popular, apart from seeming so obvious? A significant reason in the politics and economics of the education industry is that sounding out can be reduced to small steps, prepackaged in instructional materials, dealt out one bit at a time, and tested and monitored every step of the way. With sounding out, teachers and students can be publicly "held accountable" for learning. Without sounding out, teachers have to be trusted to exercise their professional expertise and judgment.

There's much more of an argument that could be made, citing masses of linguistic and educational evidence, books, professional articles, and research. But people aren't persuaded to change their minds by being assailed by evidence. If anything, evidence aggravates them.

Persuasion is a psychological challenge. Just watch the way advertisers do it. People must feel open, comfortable, and interested, not defensive. Don't tell them they're wrong; tell them there's a better way, a different story, that could solve problems for them. Tell them this *matters*, and that they could change lives. We're not talking about abstract theories, but about how children are treated in school, and whether they are helped or handicapped.

Suggest that skeptics try to read aloud just by sounding out letters (as opposed to recognizing entire words). Better still, suggest they observe children and teachers, to see whether sounding out or the alternative creates the least confusion.

Some people will never be convinced. We have to live with them. But their inability to look beyond the obvious doesn't mean they should dictate how children are taught to read.

CHAPTER SIX

A FEDERAL FETISH

Despite its manifest inadequacies, phonics has achieved the status of a fetish, an object of irrational reverence and obsessive devotion, in the higher realms of educational policy making.

In the 1980s the interminable debate on the teaching of reading focused on a federally commissioned report entitled *Becoming a Nation of Readers* (Anderson, Hiebert, Scott, and Wilkinson 1985), whose conclusions favored heavy early phonics instruction. The report was castigated in the following manner by the editor of the International Reading Association's annual review of reading research (Weintraub 1986): "There's no guarantee that the big name is synonymous with quality. Even when well-funded and headed by a blue ribbon committee, a supposedly comprehensive review may be narrowly based, considerably less than comprehensive, and biased in its election of what is included and what is excluded. . . . I happen to concur that a very selective body of literature was included and some rather critical research excluded" (vi).

The book *Beginning to Read*, by Marilyn Jager Adams (1990), was commissioned by the U.S. Department of Education following a request by Congress for an examination of the role of phonics in reading instruction. It is frequently referred to by both sides of the debate. Adams acknowledges the difficulty and unnaturalness of breaking down speech into separate sounds and relating these sounds to spellings. She notes how difficult and laborious phonics and word recognition instruction is for children before they are experienced readers, and observes specifically that "spelling-sound relationships are not the basis of reading skills and knowledge" (10). But she ends with the remarkable conclusion that the symbol-sound system should be taught explicitly and early, together with phonemic awareness training. Dorothy Strickland and Bernice Cullinan, two members of a panel set up by the Center for the Study of Reading to advise Adams, felt constrained to declare polite but firm disagreement in an Afterword published with the volume. They were particularly concerned by the emphasis on phonics, the references to children who have not yet begun to receive instruction as "prereaders" rather than "emergent readers," the selection of studies, interpretation of research, and the amount of research that took place in decontextualized situations. A similar controversy followed another federally commissioned report by Snow, Burns, and Griffin (1998) entitled *Preventing Reading Difficulties in Young Children*, which presented similar conclusions.

Possibly the mother of all educational conflicts was ignited by the report of a third federal body, the National Reading Panel (2000), whose main publication was entitled *Teaching Children to Read: An Evidence-Based Assessment of the Scientific Research Literature on Reading and its Implications for Reading Instruction*. The terms "evidence-based" and "scientific research" in the title are significant. The report is voluminous, but there is a 35-page summary. The conclusions once again are a familiar catalog of recommendations stressing direct instruction of phonics and phonemic awareness skills. Any attempt to examine the content of the report and of opposing arguments in detail would simply be a further repetition of the interminable debate. But two unique characteristics of the report have wider implications. The first was the panel's decision to partition all research on reading into two categories: *scientific*—which in practice means supportive of the phonics point of view—and *unscientific*—which means everything else. The distinction has extensive consequences ranging from the funding of literacy research to the professional status of individual teachers and professors of education. The distinction was used to justify the panel's own decision that of over 100,000 research reports that came before them, only 428 warranted close attention, and of these only 38 were used as a basis for their conclusions. The second unique characteristic was the panel's political stance. The recommendations were prescriptive, and were quickly mandated by federal and many state administrations as the sole basis of instruction for students in school and teachers at faculties of education, as well as for participants in inservice training.

Vehement criticism of the report and its conclusions followed immediately, starting with the only teacher of reading on the panel, Joanne Yatvin. She wrote a minority report which was not published or referred to in the summary, but subsequently appeared in an academic journal under the title *Babes in the Woods: The Wanderings of the National Reading Panel* (Yatvin 2002). Yatvin believes the members of the panel "lost their integrity" because government agencies at all levels are using the "science" of a flawed report to support changes in school instruction and teacher education. The titles of some related publications succinctly indicate the tenor of their contents: *Misreading Reading: The Bad Science That Hurts Children* (Coles 2000); *Reading the Naked Truth: Literacy, Legislation, and Lies* (Coles 2003); *Resisting Reading Mandates: How to Triumph With the Truth* (Garan 2002); *Literacy as Snake Oil: Beyond the Quick Fix* (Larson 2001); "Reading Between the Lines" (Metcalf 2002); and "The Politics of Phonics" (Paterson 2002). Articles by Yatvin, Garan, Paterson, and others are printed or reprinted in *Big Brother and the National Reading Curriculum: How Ideology Trumped Evidence* (Allington 2002).

The National Reading Panel report became the basis of the "Reading First Initiative" of the "No Child Left Behind" Act passed by the U.S. Congress in 2002. Later in the same year, the annual convention of the National Council of Teachers of English (NCTE) passed a resolution urging Congress to review the initiative because of professional concerns of teachers. The resolution in part declares: "This Initiative is the culmination of a recent trend, as the federal government has increasingly attempted to define what reading is, what counts as research on reading, and to dictate how reading should be taught in our classrooms. As a consequence, the government is channeling educational funding to a few corporate purveyors of a limited set of methods for teaching reading."

Three specific reasons were given why the teachers considered the initiative potentially harmful to children: individually unique children suffer when subjected to a uniform model of reading instruction; children are deprived of sensitive, responsive precision in teaching when a rigid methodology is imposed; and teaching that is based upon a limited inadequate research base risks miseducating children about reading (NCTE 2002).

My personal view of all the panels is that they share two common but misguided characteristics: (1) an obsessive approach to the alphabet and letter-sound relationships, and (2) a conviction that children will only learn when given explicit instruction. Others might add strong elements of commercial, political, or fundamentalist bias. Do I have a better idea? I think this is a case where ultimate truth is unattainable. But anyone who objectively studies language and observes children can see that characteristics (1) and (2) are both wrong. It is not difficult to see error. On the other hand, I would not presume to speculate upon "what really happens in the head." Scans of various kinds may show activity in different regions of the brain at different times, but they no more explain reading than they explain consciousness, attention, awareness, or any other mental state. Some scientists (real scientists) believe we may never resolve such issues because we don't (and perhaps can't) ask the right questions; our organized perceptions of gross events in the physical world don't relate to quantum events in the physical brain in any way that we can comprehend (see Cohen and Schooler 1997). The brain can never understand itself. This doesn't mean that we are helpless victims of ignorance or that anything goes; it means that we should avoid the pursuit of fictions and respect what can be unambiguously observed about the behavior, capacities, and feelings of people. Such an attitude won't end the interminable controversy, but it should take us beyond it.

VOICES OFF

So many experts—and you and a few others say they are all wrong. Couldn't you be the ones in error, and these highly qualified national authorities be right?

They must be right, if reading is the unnatural activity, subordinate to spoken language, that they all believe it is. From that simple premise, everything else follows. But if you happen not to believe that reading is an unnatural activity, then everything these specialized panels have concluded must be wrong. It wouldn't be the first time that nationally appointed commissions have been wrong, sometimes catastrophically so. This is not altogether the fault of the people on these commissions—they've been handpicked for what they believe—for their "area of expertise"—and the conclusions they reach are predictable. Handpick a different group of people, and you'll get opposite but equally predictable conclusions. The fault, if you want to lay blame, is on the government functionaries who set up the commissions, nominate the members, and allocate the tasks. They listen to advice, of course, only from people who have a congenial point of view. It's a closed circle. No one recommends anyone for a position of influence in a body that is supposed to reach conclusions within a certain range (Joanne Yatvin, cited above, was obviously a mistake). It would have made major headlines if the National Reading Panel had come out in favor of a philosophy that rejected everything that politicians and publishers have huge investments in.

Jeanne Chall, who launched the term "The Great Debate" in the subtitle of her classic book *Learning to Read* (Chall 1967), was fully aware of the gulf between the two points of view. In a 1992/1993 article, she declared, "Whole language proponents tend to view learning to read as a natural process, developing in ways similar to [spoken] language. Therefore, like [spoken] language, most whole language proponents say it is not necessary to teach reading directly. Direct instruction models, on the other hand, view reading as needing to be taught, and taught systematically" (8). She cites the existence of many illiterate individuals as evidence that reading is not "natural" and needs to be taught, adding: "Generally, direct instruction models favor the systematic teaching and learning of the relationships of sounds and symbols. This goes under many names—phonics, decoding, phonological awareness, word analysis, word attack, phonetic analysis, sound-symbol relations, etc." (8).

I have to say I agree with Chall's analysis, except for her belief that the existence of illiterate individuals is evidence that reading isn't natural. Many things, including the chronic absence of reading material and inappropriate instruction, can inhibit literacy. And it will take a long time for me to be persuaded that you, my reader, right now, are engaging in an unnatural activity.

If you're right, why are schools organized the way they are?

The traditional model of schooling—spare the rod and spoil the child—is based on the belief that children will do everything they can to avoid learning. They are naturally wicked. They need to be kept on task, which means that tasks must constantly be found for them. The industrial revolution systematized this model, organizing classrooms like production plants, clustering children into age and ability groups, and treating them as if they were on a production line, requiring them to engage in unison on activities that might not be questioned. Teachers were subjected to similar constraints, while expected to play the role of foreman. The alphabet was obvious, therefore it should be taught. The system has always been a dismal failure, except on the occasions when a talented teacher or student rises above the constraints. Attempts to remedy the situation have always come from outside the school, led by politicians, administrators, journalists, systems engineers, and others who have never really bothered to think about learning or reading, being quite comfortable with anything that seems obvious to them. Consistency is valued much higher than flexibility; specificity more than sensitivity.

So there's nothing I can do?
There's a lot you can do, starting with being honest with yourself and your students. If you see a child bewildered, anxious, or resentful because of what is being done in the name of education, forced into confusing or demeaning situations, then you can stop blaming the child (or the child's parents), and start looking critically at what the child is asked to do. Talk to the child about it. If you can't avoid the intrusion, then explain it. Explain that someone outside the classroom has determined what you should do. Children understand arbitrary demands and pointless restrictions—they're used to them. What they don't understand is being told that demands and restrictions are good for them, and will make them into more competent people. Above all, make sure plenty of books and other reading materials are always available.

Krashen (1993) is an unfailing advocate of "free voluntary reading" and reading for pleasure, in any genre including comic books and popular romances. He claims that most people are able to read and write—there is no "literacy crisis"—but many don't do so very well, not for want of instruction but because of lack of experience. He deplores the fact that many public and school libraries are closed or starved for funds which are relatively plentiful for more structured kinds of reading instruction and tests. Krashen and another popular free-reading crusader, Jim Trelease, are so anxious to see children have the maximum encouragement to read that they have proposed that school libraries follow the model of commercial bookstores and facilitate eating and drinking among the books (Trelease and Krashen 1996). They pre-emptively respond to predictable objections.

Elley and Mangubhai (1983) report great success in third-world countries with a "book flood" program, based on the premise that children can overcome the disadvantages of inadequate exposure to reading and poor motivation if their classrooms are flooded with high-interest illustrated reading books and the teacher helps them to read together. An updated, expanded discussion of widespread adoption in Fiji, Niue, Singapore, and South Africa, was presented in a paper by Elley (1996).

You still haven't told me how I teach a child to read who isn't interested in reading.
I can't, you can't, and you shouldn't be forced to try. Your constant concern must be to interest and reassure your students. A child coerced into reading—worse, into meaningless "pre-reading"—with punitive consequences for "failure," will only learn that reading is a mystery, school is aversive, and teachers are agents of tyranny.

CHAPTER SEVEN

SO HOW *DO* YOU IDENTIFY A NEW WORD?

When you look at a line of print your immediate experience is a meaningful event. There is no "decoding" of written words to the sounds of words, or to speech. Reading, normally, is a silent affair, just as we normally recognize houses, cars, people, and other aspects of a street scene without having to say a name for everything we encounter. Our understanding of the situation is immediate. Actual names are usually irrelevant for our understanding (unless we are telling someone else about the experience, in which case we put words to our understanding). We don't have to say the words first in order to get the meanings, the understanding.

The same applies to reading. We don't have to say to ourselves, or to anyone else, what a word is in order to understand that word. The understanding has to come first. Saying the word is something extra you do in order to recite what you read to yourself, in an "inner voice," or aloud to someone else.

But the questions always arises, "What about words you've never met before? If you don't use phonics, how do you learn to recognize those words, and how do you learn to say them?" The question usually means, "How do I *teach* children to identify and say words they have never met before?" Teachers often feel they have to find things to *do*, to instruct children, rather than arrange situations where the desired learning will take care of itself.

I'll discuss the issue in three steps: (1) summarizing how text is understood when the words are familiar, in silent reading and in reading aloud, (2) explaining how unfamiliar words are understood, and (3) explaining how unfamiliar words are read aloud.

HOW FAMILIAR WORDS ARE UNDERSTOOD

In silent reading, which is the normal and natural way to read, the words in their sequence and setting are interpreted immediately. We move directly from the words to their combined meaning, with no analysis or transformation into any aspect of spoken language. We understand the printed words *The dog jumped over the fence* the way we would understand a picture of a dog jumping over a fence, without having to say to ourselves, "The dog jumped over a fence." The sounds of the words are irrelevant.

In reading aloud, for our own purposes or to other people, an extra step is required. First we have to understand what we are reading, then we have to say what we understand. We don't transform the uninterpreted words (or their component letters) into sound; we put sound to the words that we have interpreted. We do this in exactly the same way that we identify the dog that we see jumping the fence. We don't say, "There's a dog," and then understand that it is a dog that we have seen. We recognize a dog, and then say the word that we have for animals that we recognize as dogs.

The problem in all of this, as I explained in Chapter 1, is that it is so difficult to escape the fascination of the alphabet, to overcome the apparently self-evident fact that words are comprised of letters—just as buildings may be made of bricks— therefore the sounds the letters represent must have something to do with reading (although individual bricks have nothing to do with our recognition of buildings.) Where possible I prefer to talk about the *structure* of written words, which happens to consist of letters, rather than talk about letters. No one expects structure to decode to sound.

HOW UNFAMILIAR WORDS
ARE UNDERSTOOD

I am talking now about *understanding*, not about reading aloud or about transposing written language into silent speech to ourselves. How do we get the meaning of an unfamiliar word before we even try to say it? The answer is that the meaning comes from the context in which the word occurs. Words we do know indicate the meaning of the word we don't know. Or rather, the entire grammatical and semantic structure of the meaningful sequence in which the unknown word is embedded, together often with cues within the structure of the unknown word itself (words that look alike tend to share similar meanings), enmeshes the unknown word in a network of understanding, so that the probable meaning is immediately apparent. And if we make a mistake, the later meaningful context usually tells us that our assumption was wrong, and probably suggests a more appropriate interpretation. In brief, we get the meaning of one small part from the meaning of the whole (just as you would have little difficulty inferring the meaning of the word *glerp* if I told you I left my glerp at home this morning and got soaked by rain later in the day).

There is substantial evidence that readers quickly become extremely proficient at attributing the correct meaning to unfamiliar words in the normal course of reading, not just experienced adult readers, but students in high school and even younger ones. One encounter with an unfamiliar word in a meaningful context is enough to give an approximate meaning; half a dozen encounters are sufficient to draw an accurate conclusion. In this way, readers can learn thousands of new words every year.

It is a perfectly natural thing to do. Children from the second year of their lives accurately infer the meaning of new spoken words about twenty times a day, with no forgetting—both from the language itself and the situation in which it occurs. Someone says, "Like a drink of blunk?", holds out a glass of orange juice, and the child knows what blunk is. Children do this without instruction from adults or visits to a dictionary. This is the way vocabularies grow, in spoken and written language. But it applies only to words that occur in meaningful contexts, either spoken or written; it does not apply to words that are presented in lists or in any other contrived instructional context. As I frequently reiterate, we learn when we understand; learning is a byproduct of understanding. In effect, children learn about language the way archaeologists decipher ancient texts, by bringing sense to them.

If the meaning of the unfamiliar word that we have identified is already in our spoken language vocabulary, then we can associate the written word with the spoken word, the sight with the sound. The association is mediated by meaning. Our inner "lexicon" is not a list of the sounds of words with meanings attached; it is a list of meanings with sounds and written forms attached. When we become familiar with the meaning of written words, we employ our lexicon of meanings, to establish a relationship between the written word and its spoken counterpart. The sequence is

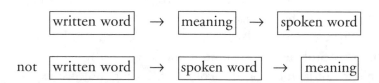

If the written word has a meaning that we *can't* associate with a spoken word, then it remains one of those written words that we can recognize and understand without being able to put into speech (or only with a very rough approximation of what the pronunciation of the word might be). It is precisely the situation we are often in when we encounter recognizable and comprehensible symbols that we haven't put a name to, such as perhaps ⊘ & ♭ and ●.

HOW UNFAMILIAR WORDS
ARE READ ALOUD

How can we put a sound (or a name) to a word that is totally unfamiliar to us? It depends on how many words we are familiar with. Words have many structural similarities—they often begin and end with familiar patterns like *un*, *pro*, *ed*, *ing*, and *tion*. Our experience with other words has shown us how they are pronounced and also how parts of them are pronounced. We can pronounce familiar structures in unfamiliar words the same way we pronounce the same structures in familiar words. If we know the pronunciation of *convey* and *persist*, we can make a good attempt at the pronunciation of *consist*, especially if we can take meaning and grammatical structure into account as well. This is not the use of phonics, which we have seen in Chapter 4 could not possibly work, nor does it demand prior learning of the parts of words in isolated exercises. All it demands is experience in reading. The use of analogies to indicate both meaning and sound is natural and automatic (provided "guessing" hasn't been inhibited).

The system is not perfect, but no system for putting sounds to unfamiliar words could be perfect. Linguists recognize that the spelling of words doesn't even attempt to indicate aspects of speech that the reader/speaker might be expected to know already. For example, everyone knows—unconsciously— from their patterns of speech that the past tense ending *ed* is pronounced /d/ at the end of words like *pulled*, but that it is pronounced /t/ at the end of words like *walked*, while in words like *handed* it is pronounced like /id/. Final *s* is pronounced /s/ at the end of words like *cups* but /z/ at the end of words like *beds*. None of this has anything to do with phonics, which doesn't acknowledge these distinctions. The difference comes from our knowledge (unconsciously acquired) of subtle and specialized rules of spoken language. The component letters of written words also tell us nothing about the intonation, whether for example the stress falls at the beginning, as in *a*corn, or at the end, as in a*bout*.

We recognize new and unfamiliar words because of what we already know of words that are familiar. We can put meanings and pronunciations to them because of what we know about spoken words that have a similar appearance.

All this takes place very rapidly. Researchers have found that "fast mapping" of a tentative meaning takes place on the first encounter with a new word, and half a dozen more encounters suffice to fully round out the conventional meaning—with no "feedback" beyond the context in which the word occurs. For the sounds of written words the mapping is just as fast, if bothered with at all. The sounds are not always correct—we get the meaning but mispronounce the conventional sounds for words we haven't encountered in speech. Such words may then go into our spoken language vocabulary with an inappropriate pronunciation, to be corrected fairly rapidly if we hear the word spoken, but otherwise to remain idiosyncratic.

How do we get the *correct* pronunciation? Either someone tells us how the word is pronounced at a helpful time, or we subsequently hear the word spoken and make the connection to the word we have encountered in our reading. Nothing about finding meanings and pronunciations for new words is normally a *problem* for learners, only for people who think that writing is a visible form of speech, rather than that writing and speech are related but independent forms of language.

Neither the sounds of letters nor words themselves are represented in speech the way they are in writing. If we didn't have a writing system we wouldn't know what words are, and no one would try to break down the flowing intermingling sounds of speech into individual segments like letters. Only meaning can be common to spoken and written language, and meaning is not something that can be decomposed into segments in any form of language.

CHAPTER EIGHT

JUST A MATTER OF TIME

Like many people, I know a child who is having trouble in school. I'll call him John.

There's nothing wrong with John, as far as I can tell, though his school authorities are subjecting him to all kinds of diagnostic tests. The results of these tests, and the conclusions drawn from them, will go into his school record. A label is also being attached to John that could affect his future as well as his perception of himself.

The label says that John can't keep up. That's the polite version. Other versions identify him as a slow learner, a disabled learner, a probable malingerer, insufficiently motivated, and attentionally disordered. John gets upset by all the derogatory things said about him, by his continual frustration in class, and by the cajoling or disciplinary pressure his beleaguered parents put on him at home when his friends are out playing. Because he gets upset in this way, John is also categorized as being emotionally and behaviorally dysfunctional.

Things aren't getting better for John. He is falling further behind and he is expected to work even harder to keep up. He has to do more work than other students, the work is harder for him than for other students, and he gets less of the teacher's attention (and less of the teacher's praise). He sees a tutor every week. Students like John exasperate teachers, who can also fall behind in the expectations for *their* work.

John's latest report card is full of Ds and negative remarks, with imperatives like "he must," "he needs," "he should," and disparagements like "major difficulties," "many problems," and "limited strategies." There are frequent references to how hard it is for John to understand the work he is required to do, but no suggestion that the school might do anything to make his work more comprehensible to him. If John finds the work hard, that's his problem. His parents are required to acknowledge and comment upon the report, and a note at the bottom reminds them that the original of the report will be retained in John's official records until five years after he leaves school (which means that every teacher he encounters in the future will first read of his perceived inadequacies). John's parents have two other children who also make calls on their time with homework and family activities, while the parents are trying to be substitute teachers for John. (And parents need their downtime too.)

I don't like to contemplate what will happen if John's present goodwill erodes and he gets angry about what is being done to him, or thinks about school as negatively as school thinks about him.

Like the gap between the rich and the poor, and between rich countries and poor countries, the gap in school achievement between the students who can keep up, and those like John who can't, gets wider. Catching up gets harder, not easier.

Yet John has only one problem, as far as I can see. He sometimes needs more time. Give him more time, and he could do everything the other students can do.

I don't think that because John sometimes needs more time there must be something wrong with him. All human beings operate at different speeds. We all differ in the amount of time we need to sleep at night, get up in the morning, eat a meal, contribute to a discussion, read a book, write a letter, walk a mile, or learn a skill. Some people are faster than other people, at some things at least, which means that other people are slower. So it goes. But even if there were something wrong with John, the remedy would be the same. He needs more time.

The need for more time is universal. Many adults are afflicted by it, but they can usually escape the pressing situation, for brief periods at least. John has no hope of relief. He has to go to school, where "falling behind" is a constant hazard, and he is required to take home the work he hasn't finished at school, curtailing his stress-releasing playtime. Students of all ages and abilities are expected to achieve arbitrary targets and objectives, and they are put into a competitive relationship with each other where winners and losers are both inevitable and predictable.

So why can't John be given more time?

WHY TIME IS SHORT

The first excuse for giving John less time than he needs is usually a restatement of the problem. The school day and the school year are organized in such a tightly structured way that there is no extra time available. For John to spend more time on one thing would mean less time for him to do others. Everything must run on time.

It is difficult to find an equivalent situation outside school. Planes run late, ships run aground, buses run off the road, and trains run into each other. The transportation system copes. Judges are indisposed, witnesses fail to turn up, and lawyers lose their files, but the legal system survives. No one has to rush for years to catch up. Concerts are canceled, hurricanes strike, businesses fail, and empires crumble. But life goes on. Victims usually get help, or at least sympathy. They're not usually held accountable for their misfortunes.

Saying there is not enough time for John makes it clear what the problem is. John is not the problem, he is a casualty. The problem is the way the educational system structures time, so there is not enough of it for John and the other students like him. It is like depriving students of air and then blaming them for not breathing fast enough.

The second excuse for John's time bind is that you have to have standards. But what is the use of standards if it is impossible for some people to achieve them? It's one thing to specify a *communal* goal that as many children as possible reach a certain standard, but quite another matter to impose a *personal* goal to require individuals to meet those standards, and in a limited amount of time, no matter how difficult it might be for them.

The teachers are in their own time bind. Their day is structured by a detailed curriculum, test schedules, and the daily lesson plans they are required to follow. It is perhaps natural for many of them to try to pass this pressure on to their students and to the parents of their students. John is a problem for his teacher, but he is not the cause of the teacher's problems. The cause is the arbitrary constraints of the system in which the teacher is expected to operate.

It is argued that you can't hold everyone back just because a few students fall behind. But if you expect everyone to advance together, then such a dilemma is inevitable. The speed of a convoy is determined by the slowest ship. During hostilities, an emergency solution might be to abandon or sink the slowest ship, but that is scarcely a good model for education. A productive alternative would be to accept that some ships will reach the destination later than others. All that really matters is to keep them safe and seaworthy.

It is argued that some students fall behind because they are lazy or perverse; they should shape up. Possibly. But to regard all students who fall behind as candidates for boot camp discipline is not only unfair, it makes life even harder for them. John has no illusions about his situation; he would love to catch up.

It is also argued that we live in a tough and competitive world, and students should come to terms with this fact as part of their education. But even if such an attitude were defensible, there would be no reason to break the spirits of children prematurely. The people best able to survive food shortages are those who have been adequately fed through their lives, not those who have been systematically starved.

Suppose all students could be given the time and help they need to complete the tasks that were expected of them? This seemingly ideal solution sometimes arouses the biggest objection of all—that it wouldn't be fair to the students who are able to get their work done on time.

I encountered this rationale at first hand in South Africa a few years ago. Black university students, outstanding in all ways except for their familiarity with academic English, were constantly failed because they were unable to complete their English language assignments and examinations on time. Why not give them more time, I asked? Because that would be unfair to the white students, I was told. Of course, such an attitude was not surprising in the land that produced apartheid. But should there be a similar objection in North America?

What does all this boil down to? Time is short because it is arbitrarily restricted. John can't get more time because the people who determine the school day won't give it to him. And in expecting John to do what he is required to do in less time than he needs, teachers and parents are recruited to share responsibility for John's tardiness. They are persuaded that he could keep up if he—and they—really tried. John's difficulties are publicized as the failures of "accountable" teachers and parents. He, his parents, his teacher, and his school bear the mark of his transgression as conspicuously as a scarlet letter.

WHAT CHANGES COULD BE MADE?

It would be unrealistic to expect the entire educational system to change, certainly not in time to help John, though it is the system that is the root cause of his problem. But changes of attitude are a necessary beginning for both immediate relief and long-term improvement.

The first requirement is a change of attitude toward John. The labeling should go. There should be less pressure, not more. Rather than pretending that some superhuman effort will enable John to catch up with his peers (in which case another child would take over his position), everything should be done to maintain John's respect for himself. People who are not great athletes or great artists don't usually feel ashamed of the fact.

Second, there should be a change of attitude toward teachers and parents. Parents shouldn't feel guilt for the failure of their child to maintain a pace set for speedier students, and teachers shouldn't be held accountable for children unable to achieve goals set by some distant authority. Unreasonable pressure on parents and teachers frequently finds its way to the child, when instead they should be protecting the child. A more relaxed regime at home and at school might result in John learning far more than he can achieve at present.

John's plight frequently puts his teacher and his parents into conflict with each other. Understanding and acknowledgment of the underlying educational problem could help the adults as well as John. And parents and teachers working together could help bring about the political and attitudinal changes through which the educational system itself might be reformed.

There should be much more respect for all children, starting with the recognition that they have no choice about going to school. (I don't consider home schooling a solution to John's problem, because it is not always available, because schools offer—or should offer—superior facilities, and because home-schooled children can be put under just as much pressure as those in the classroom.)

It is easy to sentimentalize—that teachers love their students, that many children (the ones who can keep up) love school, and that schools protect children as well as educate them. It is in schools that children learn to be good citizens, and to respect themselves and each other.

But schools are not democratic institutions. The only comparable situations in the adult world, where people are forced to be where they are and to do what they are told, is judicial confinement in a prison or conscription into the armed services. By law, child labor is prohibited. But "work" is the most common word for what children are expected to do in school, in conditions that would be considered archaic in many adult workplaces. They usually can't chat to a neighbor or wander around the room; they can't eat, drink, or go to the toilet when they want to; and they are talked about in demeaning and discriminatory ways that would be regarded as an affront to the human rights of adults. They are forced to compete, to sit for tests that can last hours at a stretch, and to conform. I'm talking of children, or of teenagers, in their most vulnerable years as they strive to define their own identities and their relationships to society.

If we can't immediately change the educational system, we should protect those students who have difficulty with it. Instead of saying, "Sorry, kid, you don't fit the school," we should say, "Sorry, kid, the school doesn't fit you," acknowledging what the problem is. Perhaps we should tell John: "You've got to go through the car wash, but we'll do our best to protect you from bruising and demoralization." Ideally, no student would fail, because failure would be an alien concept in an educational system. Being unable to keep up should be regarded as no more reprehensible than failing to get on a train that is already leaving the station. Doing your best is all you can do.

A LONG-TERM PERSPECTIVE

But perhaps it is time to take a radical new look at education. The present system is about 150 years old, introduced about the same time that the technology of industrial efficiency was putting hens into batteries and cattle into confinement sheds. It was a production-line model with living creatures as the raw materials. Start every bird or animal (or child) at the same place, treat it in the same way under closely controlled and monitored conditions, and the final product will be of an identical standard (Smith 1998).

Of course, schools are constantly being changed, but always with the aim of making them more efficient, not more humane. That is why all centralized educational reforms focus on tests and accountability. Politicians and administrators, interested in costs and results, try to make the system we have work better, not differently.

Since the original introduction of the battery system into classrooms, grouping children according to age and expected ability, we have forgotten what schools are for and how people learn. The old idea, which we still take for granted in everyday life, is that people learn from experience. Everything you do leaves its mark on you. The new idea, which dominates education and business, is that people learn by acquiring information.

The failure of the information acquisition approach is that the rote learning of facts is the most difficult way to learn and the most common cause of forgetting. Learning facts is no guarantee of retention or of wisdom. And drills do not help children learn reading, writing, mathematics, or anything else unless there is an underlying understanding, which then makes the drills unnecessary. But the information acquisition approach assumes that understanding inevitably follows, although the opposite is the case.

Experience is responsible for almost all the learning we do in life, both the desirable and the undesirable. Through his current experience in school, John is learning what he can't do, and that he is a failure. Instead, what he needs from school are positive and productive experiences.

What should be important is not that every learner assimilate a specific amount of history, chemistry, mathematics, or literature, the precise components of which are always arbitrary, but that the learner have an opportunity to *experience* history, chemistry, mathematics, or literature. The learning of skills and acquisition of knowledge follows from the development of interest in a subject. Forcing anyone to learn skills when there is no interest in or familiarity with the subject usually results in permanent failure and antipathy.

In the world outside school, children are given the opportunity to become acquainted with hockey (and to play it in their imaginations as well as on the ice or in the street) before they are committed—hopefully with their consent—to learn and practice specific skills. Fortunate children get the opportunity to become acquainted with reading, with music, and with scientific topics from astronomy to zoology, before these become formal academic subjects. The best teachers, inside school and out, are the ones who make subjects interesting and comprehensible. We all know the influence that other children have on what our own children learn, simply by engaging them in interesting experiences.

A major difference between the experience and the information and skills approaches is that experience isn't measured by tests. One reason there is such an emphasis today on teaching specific bits of information and isolated elements of skills is precisely because they are testable and countable.

Schools should be places where interesting experiences are always available, where scientists are doing science, artists doing art, craftspeople doing craft, and everyone is behaving in a democratic and civil manner. Not all teachers need have the same skills—they could bring visitors into their classrooms and learn with their students. The important thing would be for teachers to have genuine and communicable interests in the kinds of experiences they are expected to provide. They would be mentors, not managers, and students would have the opportunity to participate in any activity without discrimination or recrimination. No one would be short of time.

Everything taught in specific subject areas today is at the expense of other things in those areas. All learning is a sampling. No arbitrary set of "basics" in science, music, literature, art, "life skills," or citizenship is going to give a student fundamental abilities or interests in those areas. But experience in any aspect of science, music, literature, art, "life skills," or citizenship provides opportunities to learn and feel what the full extent of possibilities might be. Such opportunities offer inclusion, not exclusion; free-range learning, not the battery system.

Reading, writing, and basic arithmetic come with experience. Understanding of literature, science, and civics comes with participation. In *"Surely You're Joking, Mr. Feynman!,"* Nobel prizewinning physicist Richard Feynman (1985) declared that it wouldn't matter if many aspects of science were neglected completely, provided children at some time had the opportunity to think like scientists. Specific areas of expertise could be developed when necessary, provided the initial involvement and interest had been established.

Such an approach would solve a lot of problems. For a start, administrators could stop struggling to standardize everything in schools. Instead, variety would be desirable. There would be no problem of students failing to keep up, or of being held back. Students could help each other rather than competing. There would be less reason for cheating or for plagiarism. There would be no problem because of unavoidable absence, or of moving from one school to another. And time would not be in short supply.

There would be no need for the distractions of teaching to tests, administering tests, and helping children to recover from tests. It would be easier to recruit parents into participation in the education of their own and other children. The purpose of education would become obvious and it would be easier to detect and rectify schools' failure to provide possibilities of experience.

This may sound simplistic and too easy. It would in fact be difficult, but only because it requires thinking about schools in a radically different way. It is nothing more than historical bad luck that we have the regressive education system that we do. But there is no reason that we can't go forward with a dramatic change, the way that flying machines became a practical possibility when inventors rejected the "obvious" idea that planes would have to flap their wings.

The idea of education through experience is not a new idea, even in contemporary life. There are innumerable environments in the world outside school where learning takes place through supportive, noncoercive, and collaborative activities. We call them societies, associations and clubs (Smith 1988).

The change won't happen overnight, but even if we just begin to reflect on the possibility of alternatives to schools as they are today, we could begin to change the attitudes and practices that give John such a hard time. We should at least have time for that.

CHAPTER NINE

GOING BANANAS WITH MATHEMATICS

Reading is not the only area of education where unspeakable acts and unnatural practices abound. They are rife in the direct instruction of mathematics, particularly in the early grades, where children may be required to read, or to listen to, as much nonsensical material as in reading instruction. The consequences can be just as lasting and intellectually stifling.

Here's one mathematical issue in a nutshell. A teacher points to a picture, one of many on a page or on a computer monitor, something like this:

$$\text{🍌🍌} + \text{🍌🍌🍌} = \text{🍌🍌🍌🍌🍌}$$

and says, "Here are two bananas and here are three more bananas, and two bananas plus three bananas makes five bananas. Can't you see? Count them for yourself." (The demonstration may also take place with other kinds of fruit, ducks, or dinosaurs; wooden blocks and pencils are popular for old-fashioned manual demonstrations.)

The problem is that while it is obvious to the teacher that two bananas and three bananas makes five bananas, the student may have no idea what the teacher is talking about (even if the child can count up to ten). The unhappy collision of miscommunication can leave both teacher and student frustrated and unhappy. What neither realizes is that when the teacher or the text says, "Two bananas and three bananas makes five bananas," they are not using everyday language. What the teacher is trying to say is unspeakable in everyday language, and what the child is expected to understand is an unnatural practice.

A TALE OF TWO WORLDS

Numbers don't exist in the familiar physical world around us, in the world of bananas, pencils, trees, cows, and automobiles. There are bananas, but not numbers of bananas, just as bigger or better bananas don't exist except in relation to other bananas, in comparisons we make in our own mind. Bigness, like threeness or fiveness, is a concept that we impose upon the physical world. When we find numbers anywhere it is because we have put them there; the numbers have come from somewhere else.

Where have the numbers come from? The world of mathematics. This is a different world, though it can be explored just like the familiar world around us, and there are lots of discoveries that can be made in it. They both have their own language. The meanings of our everyday language lie in the world around us; the meanings of the language of mathematics lie in the world of mathematics. The languages are different; they are used to say different things. But unfortunately they sound the same.

The world of mathematics is not the only world human beings can inhabit that is different from the familiar physical world. Another significant world of its own is the world of music, which also has its own language. There are other worlds as well; it is interesting to reflect on what they might be.

Why do I insist on talking about *different* worlds that have *different* languages? Because you can't translate statements from one world to another.

A phrase of music can't be converted into a mathematical expression, or into everyday words. I wouldn't get very far with this explanation if I tried to play it on the piano, or sum it up in a few equations. To appreciate music you have to experience it from within the world of music. To understand mathematics you have to be located within the world of mathematics. Everyday language won't get you anywhere in either of those situations.

Here is a sentence in everyday language:

The bananas are green.

Here is a sentence in mathematical language:

Five is a prime number.

Here is a sentence in a mixture of everyday and mathematical language:

Here are five bananas.

What does the word *five* mean in the previous sentence? It means precisely what the teacher asserts in saying that two plus three equals five—but that has nothing to do with bananas. The meaning of any number is all the relationships it can have with other numbers. The meaning of 5 is 2 + 3, 4 + 1, 6 − 1, 8 − 3, 10/2, the square root of 25, and innumerable other possibilities. And all of these meanings are universal, far more than any word or concept in our everyday language. On any other planet and in the farthest reaches of the cosmos, 5 would still be a prime number and the square root of 25.

And all of this is a consequence of the way numbers are defined in the first place, that one more than one is two, one more than two is three, one more than three is four (which is also 2 × 2, 4 × 1, and 5 − 1). From such a simple beginning, all of the innumerable possible and totally dependable truths of mathematics are generated. And none of them can be found in the physical world, on Mars or Jupiter, or anywhere in the furthest reaches of the cosmos. They can only be found, explored, and exploited in the world of mathematics.

That is why the banana example is futile. Unless the learner already understands what is meant by the numbers "two," "three," and "five," there is no way the learner will understand the statement.

A teacher holding up bananas and saying, "Look, there are two of them" might just as well be saying, "Look, they're yellow" to a color-blind observer. Two bananas don't *explain* twoness; the understanding has to come from the learner, who must already understand what "two" means in the language of mathematics.

Here are a couple of familiar words in everyday language that don't mean the same in mathematical language:

> What is the opposite of *more*? Everyone says *less*, except for a child who hasn't learned any mathematical language, who doesn't understand the mathematical concept of *more*. For such a child the opposite of *more* is inevitably "No more." Children whose request for more juice is denied would be surprised to find some of what they already have taken away.

> What is *zero*? It is not nothing. Often it is an arbitrary point on a scale. Zero on the Fahrenheit scale of temperature is not the same as zero on the Celsius scale (and on neither scale does zero indicate an absence of temperature). In the world of mathematics, zero is a number, which happens to fall between +1 and −1 (so zero is an even number). You can add it to and subtract it from other numbers. (There are some problems about multiplying and dividing by zero, but you can only understand those through mathematics; you can't find an explanation in the everyday world or everyday language.) The fact that you can add zero as often as you like but you can't multiply by zero so freely shows that multiplication isn't a simple matter of successive additions, which is what most children are told. The fact that multiplication by fractions makes numbers smaller, while division by fractions makes numbers bigger, is another counterintuitive fact about the world of mathematics.

MORE DOUBLE-TALK

Even the simplest of mathematics can become difficult to read and understand when precise and unambiguous mathematical expressions are "translated" into everyday language and situations. There can be no argument that $6 + 3 = 9$, that $6 - 3 = 3$, that $6 \times 3 = 18$, and that $6 \div 3 = 2$, from a mathematical point of view. The notational links can be given names—such as *plus, minus, multiply, divide,* and *equals*—and there are also many synonyms—such as *add, take away, subtract, times,* and *make.* As long as these terms are taken to refer to particular mathematical relationships—as mathematical language—there is no problem. But if the words are expected to *explain* mathematical relationships there can be considerable confusion, because natural language and the language of mathematics have different meanings.

I should reiterate that the difficulties exist only for learners and others who don't understand what people using these common mathematical terms are talking about. For anyone familiar with the mathematics, who has no trouble with addition, subtraction, multiplication, and division, the casual use of mathematical language appears obvious. Such people often wonder why beginners can have so much trouble. This is a difficulty for me as an author in writing about such matters. Readers long familiar with *plus, minus,* and all the other technical words may find it difficult to see why the ambiguities I talk about create any kind of problem. Surely their meanings are obvious. I can only suggest that such readers try to imagine the problems they would have trying to understand "simple explanations" of recondite matters they know little about, a learned discussion of quantum physics, perhaps, or microbiology, or postmodernism.

We may think we are using clear and familiar language when we ask a child to add a pair of numbers, or to take one away from another, but unless the child already understands what we are saying *mathematically,* the child won't understand what we are talking about. Explaining or illustrating how the words are used in everyday written or spoken language doesn't explain or illustrate how they are used in mathematics. I'll give a few examples.

"Add" (or "plus")

When used mathematically, the word *add* refers to a specific relationship between numbers that is essentially undefined, a pattern in mathematical space. When used in everyday contexts, *add* has quite different meanings. If a recipe tells us to add milk to cake mix it refers to a physical operation, not a mathematical one. You don't add 2 to 3 the way you add milk to a cake mix, water to cement, or love to a relationship. Pie plus ice cream is not the same as 2 + 3. Two and three don't "make" five the way that soil and water make mud, an athlete makes the team, or an assignment makes the grade. Two "plus" three has nothing in common with a hamburger plus fries, nor is it analogous to the way a hem is added to a garment or a postscript added to a piece of correspondence.

Unless you already understand the numbers two, three, and five mathematically, being shown bananas and being told they are two, three, or five is meaningless. *Two* is not the same kind of word as *yellow*, *curved*, or *fruit*.

"Minus" (or "subtract," "take away")

Minus is not a common word in everyday language, and when it is used—"Unfortunately, I'm minus my umbrella today," "I was hoping for at least an A-minus on the test"—it doesn't have anything like the mathematical meaning.

Terms such as *difference* and *take away* are frequently used, but with a sense that has nothing in common with the mathematical relationship of subtraction. The difference between 5 and 2 is not the same as the difference between baseball and football, or between apples and oranges, and 2 taken away from 5 is not the same as a toy taken away from a child or a snack taken away from a fast-food restaurant. You don't take 2 from 5 the way you take a glass from the shelf or a candy from a packet. Subtraction may be used to compute the difference between the two dollars I have and the five dollars you have, but no money actually changes hands; there is no taking away.

The "minus" explanation also doesn't help comprehension of "negative" numbers, which have the minus sign placed in front of them. There is no real-world analogy for a negative quantity of anything, even money, that doesn't involve mathematical understanding. The terms "positive" and "negative" themselves don't function in mathematics the way they do in everyday language, for example with positive and negative remarks. Numbers less than zero aren't negative in the way that an answer, a response, or an attitude is negative. A negative number doesn't mean "No." It is not negative the way an electric wire or power source might be negative (which is also an odd use of the term), nor has it anything in common with the negative of a photograph. The complexities of negative numbers can be explained to novices only in terms of mathematics.

"Multiply" (or "times")
Numbers don't multiply the way weeds or rabbits multiply. Multiplication is not repeated addition, either in mathematics or the world in general, no matter how often mathematics textbooks make the claim.

Children are usually told that "multiply" means "times"— "four times three is twelve." In normal language, however, the verb "to multiply" doesn't mean "times." It simply means "increase." The biblical injunction to "go forth and multiply" doesn't mean add to yourself a certain number of times; it means have children. Problems are multiplied when there are new ones, but not repetitions of the same problem. An official who times a sporting event is measuring, not calculating, and so is the person who says, "I've seen that movie three times already."

"Divide"
You don't divide a cake the way you divide five by three. The popular analogy of slicing a pie doesn't demonstrate what

happens when a number is divided. In everyday language, division means splitting or sharing, not necessarily in equal portions, or disconnecting a part from a whole. "United we stand, divided we fall" makes no mathematical sense.

There's a clue in the fact that dictionaries don't offer explanations for the mathematical use of any of the terms I have just listed. In one popular dictionary, for example, the definitions for the verb *to add* go through the "join," "mix," and "increase" type of definition for everyday language, but merely the vacuous "to perform mathematical addition" for the mathematical sense.

"Equals"

Perhaps the most difficult symbol of all. Mathematicians don't define it. Equals doesn't mean "the same as," "amounts to," or "the answer is." Two plus three doesn't equal five the way five candy bars equal, or are the same as, another five. In mathematics, a number of different things can be done around the = sign; for example, anything done to one side must be done to the other, and everything on one side can be replaced by everything on the other. There is nothing similar in the concept of equality in everyday language.

In the world outside mathematics, adults and children don't normally say that two things are equal if they are substitutable for each other; instead they say that things are "the same as," "as much as," "as many as," "as big as," or occasionally "can take the place of." They don't say that a cork is "equal to" a screw top for closing a bottle. Frequently used phrases like "equal rights" and "equal opportunity" have no mathematical equivalence. So what does it mean to tell a mathematical novice that two plus two equals four (or is "the same as" four, or "makes" four)? The flash of understanding—that both sides of the equation are the same number—can only come from inside mathematics.

Many other mathematical terms are used frequently in everyday language—for example, *count, number, total, place, column, solution,* and *answer*—but there is no need to belabor the point. There are many more examples, and a lot more elaboration, in *The Glass Wall: Why Mathematics Can Seem Difficult* (Smith 2002).

FAKING IT WITH DIRECT INSTRUCTION

All this linguistic confusion demonstrates that it is unrealistic to expect anyone to learn mathematics through mindless repetition and incessant drills. But this is the chosen way of direct instruction. Drill until you get it right, until correct responses become a habit (though not an understanding). That's what all those pages of worksheets are for, in mathematics as in reading. If a child labors to get 60, 70, or 80 percent of the repetitions correct, then an acceptable level of competence has been achieved. With luck, the child will be able to fake it on the test.

Drill is not what you need if you don't understand anything. It's unnatural to keep repeating something you don't understand. If I don't understand what it means to say, "The double helix of DNA consists of two intertwined sugar-phosphate chains," it doesn't help me to keep repeating the statement (though it may help me briefly to fake it for an examination or to impress other people). This is no different from memorizing phonics rules in order to pass a reading test. Some teachers become very good at helping students to fake a minimal competence—and many students become very good at doing so. But they haven't learned anything useful, and have probably acquired some detrimental habits.

The students—like the teachers—may even come to look and feel as if they are mathematicians, but they never get beyond minimal mathematical competence. They'll shudder at long division, sweat over simple statistics, and cross the street to avoid fractions and decimals. Faking ends the moment you run into the barrier of incomprehension.

SO IT'S IMPOSSIBLE TO LEARN MATHEMATICS?

A useful and enjoyable level of familiarity with mathematics is not unattainable. But it's impossible to gain it from mechanical classroom practices, from recitations, from skills sheets and practice books, and from rote memorization of a few tricks—

all unnatural practices. It's impossible to push mathematics into a child's head. You can't be *instructed* to learn mathematics. So how do children become mathematicians? By discovering (or inventing) it for themselves, just as they can with reading.

Constance Kamii knows exactly how to do it. She's a master teacher in Birmingham, Alabama, and has written three books on the topic (Kamii 1985/2000, 1989, 1994). Kamii was a student and colleague of the eminent Swiss psychologist Jean Piaget, and her educational philosophy is *constructivist* (as is the present book).

Constructivism as a philosophical theory holds that knowledge—and therefore understanding—is not a property of the physical world, but something that has to be personally constructed by each individual. Explanation doesn't create knowledge or understanding. Everything we know and think must be constructed and tested in our own mind. This is not to say that we can create any kind of knowledge that we like— we usually (though not always) test our theories against our experience and against the theories of other people. We look for coherence, consistency, and consensus. But knowledge can't be put into anyone's mind. It must come from insight and re- flection, even when we are simply thinking about something we have been told.

The constructivist stance is that mathematical understand- ing is not something that can be explained to children, nor is it a property of objects or other aspects of the physical world. There is no mathematical understanding in bananas. Instead, children must "invent" mathematics, in situations analogous to those in which relevant aspects of mathematics were invented or discovered in the first place. They must construct mathemat- ics for themselves, using the same mental tools and attitudes they employ to construct understanding of the language they hear around them. An accessible introduction to constructivism from an educational perspective is Fosnot (1995). Saxe (1991) describes constructivism in practice by untutored Brazilian street children who devise their own complex business math- ematical systems.

Kamii argues, for example, that there's no need to teach addition. First graders can construct the relevant logical mathematical knowledge on their own when engaged in such activities as equalizing small stacks of counters. She wants children to learn as a result of their own thinking, not from "facts," when involved in situations in daily living, in voting, and in board and dice games, as well as in discussions of computational problems.

Kamii refers to conventional rules for mathematical procedures, like "carrying" and "borrowing," as *algorithms,* and is highly critical of "tricks" and "algorithms" that are taught without concern for comprehension. Her research showing harmful effects of teaching algorithms in the first four grades, and compatible findings from many other parts of the world, are reported in Kamii and Dominick (1998). She shows how mastery of numbers and of numerical operations can develop spontaneously with the progression of children's "scientific thinking." And logical, scientific thinking, she argues, arises from children's *reflective abstraction* from their own actions. Kamii urges that children should be autonomous in their learning, to encourage them to think, and she also stresses the importance of social interaction. Conflicting ideas, like incorrect responses, may be necessary if higher levels of understanding are to be attained. For other volumes discussing ways in which teachers try to generate mathematical thinking through problems and discussions, see Cobb and Bauersfeld (1995) and Carpenter, Fennema, Franke, Levi, and Empson (1999).

None of this means that children should be left to their own resources to recapitulate five thousand years of mathematical history, including all of the false turns and blind alleys. But it does assert that children can and must discover mathematics for themselves if given opportunities for relevant experience and reflection. The role of the teacher, in mathematics as in reading, is: keep it interesting, don't create difficulties, recognize anxieties, and try to come from what students understand, rather than from incomprehensible definitions and unnatural activities that are meaningless to them. As with reading, engage in the desired enterprise with the child until the child is ready to take over.

I'll end with a resounding clash of language that I read in a certified scientific context—a high school biology text:

Cells divide in order to multiply.

I wonder how many students have gone bananas over that casual remark.

CHAPTER TEN

WHEN IRRESISTIBLE TECHNOLOGY MEETS IRREPLACEABLE TEACHERS

The undermining of meaningful reading experience by mindless "direct instruction" takes place at several levels. The issue is not simply the kind of activity presented to children in the name of reading; it is also how that activity is organized and controlled in the classroom. It is an issue that pits teachers against technology.

Meaningful literacy education is labor intensive. Until new readers are ready to entrust themselves to authors, living breathing people are required to provide them with guidance, help, encouragement, and reassurance. Electronic technology is not much use in providing such empathetic resources.

Direct instruction, on the other hand, finds teachers a nuisance. It tries to keep them out of the way as much as possible. It specifies in the finest detail what students must do and scripts what teachers have to say. The ideal instrument for direct instruction is a computer program.

Many such programs that claim to teach reading have been produced. They range from the cheap and amateurish to the expensive and sophisticated, but all have the same orientation—they think reading is decoding to sound, that intensive instruction in phonics and phonemic awareness is essential, and that learning to read is completing masses of drill and short-answer exercises. The more asinine the activities are, they more they are jazzed up to look like computer games and advertised as FUN!! Almost all claim to be "science-based."

I'm not debating whether computers and other electronic technology in education are good or bad; the answer is "it all depends." The issue is, who should be in charge of children's educational activities, a teacher on the spot who knows the children, can see them, and is sensitive to their needs and interests, or a group of experts and technicians, remote in time and space, who try to program children to become readers?

WHO'S RIGHT?

Many teachers welcome computers for the interesting experiences and useful activities they make possible. Other teachers fear that computers threaten their authority and possibly their existence. Which group is right?

They both are. Computers are useful tools that should not be disdained, and vehicles of social change that must not be ignored. Every technology transforms our lives, whether we want it to or not. It's natural for people to want to use technology; it's not natural when technology uses people.

Electronic technology infiltrates our lives from all directions. It dictates the shape of industry, transportation, finance, communications, medicine, agriculture, entertainment, and innumerable other critical aspects of our existence. It has already made profound changes in education. Technology always makes demands on people. We may feel we control technology because as individuals we employ it in convenient or useful ways. But as a mass we are subservient to the technology we have let into our lives. When computer systems shut down, banks, stores, airlines, and hospitals can't function. Schools may soon be in that situation.

Many teachers are concerned about what they should do with electronic technology. My concern is with what technology will do with teachers. First, however, I'll talk about the intimate relationship between people and technology. We must understand that it's usually impossible to control the development and advance of technology, even if we want to.

RECIPROCAL CONTROL

It's a mistake to lay the credit (or the blame) for all the different kinds of technology that we have today on a few exceptionally intelligent and creative individuals, without whose innovations the technology would not exist. Almost everyone is involved in the development of the technologies that fill our lives, and technologies determine their own development at least as much as humans do. People and technology are inseparable.

Technology is irresistible because people constantly strive to further their own powers. They exploit anything that enables them to see further, hear more acutely, communicate more distantly, travel faster, carry heavier loads, expand memory, write faster and more legibly, and think more effectively. Artists have always been quick to exploit opportunities offered by technology (frequently while criticizing it at the same time). As a species, we can no more give up possibilities extended by any technology than we could contemplate cutting off our legs or putting out our eyes. No technology has ever been discarded unless it was superseded by another. We do not reject technologies "for our own good." There is always someone to pick up where another person may have decided to leave off.

Technology is always developed to maximize its utility with the resources currently available—a technological survival of the fittest. The clipper ships of the nineteenth century were close to being the ultimate sailing machines, the most efficient vessels possible, given the materials that were available at the time. The passenger jet aircraft today is close to optimum levels of performance, given the current state of materials, power sources, and human tolerance for being packaged into small spaces. Modern aircraft will doubtless be superseded, but only by a more efficient technology when new resources (including finances and other technology) become available.

Machines don't design themselves, but their relationship with the humans who take advantage of them leads inexorably to refinement in their design and universalization in their use. People and their technologies coexist, and each helps to determine the manner in which the other exists.

The same applies to our institutions—to the legal system, health care, finance, and education—although they often seem slower to change, perhaps because people have differing points of view about what constitutes "improvement" for an institution. But there is reciprocal control. We change our systems and institutions as we accommodate to them. Any manner in which we—or others—organize our lives is a technology.

It doesn't matter if we as individuals don't like the way our lives are organized for us. If we persuade or prevent one group of people from interfering with our lives through systems or devices that we don't approve of, another group of people will arise to take their place. The pressure that controls our lives doesn't come from people, it comes from the technology they employ (or serve). Technology not only controls our lives, it also controls the lives of the people who control us.

LEARNING AND EDUCATION

Learning is not a technology, though teaching frequently is. The so-called learning programs and systems that abound in the commercial world, pervading education, are in fact *teaching* technologies, and teaching and learning are by no means complementary. Learning is a natural and continual function of human beings, as instinctive and ceaseless as breathing. Learning is mental growth, and like physical growth it is inevitable given a healthy and nurturing environment. The tragedy for most people, perhaps for all of us some of the time, is not that we fail to learn what we might want to learn, but that we can't help learning things that we would be better off not learning.

Learning is a *social* activity, dependent upon the way in which we construct our personal identities (Smith 1998). We learn the kind of person we are, and the kind we are not. No matter how hard we try to learn something that we have learned we *can't* learn, we inevitably fail.

Learning is natural and continual, taking place through social interactions with the people we identify with, especially through language—either in the "real world" or in books, and to a lesser extent in drama and movies, on television, and on the Internet.

What makes this identification possible? *Imagination.* We would be unable to identify with anyone, and therefore unable to learn anything except basic and brutish habits, without the unique power of the human imagination. (And imagination, of course, is central in our symbiotic relationship with technology.)

The three keys to human learning, therefore, are (1) imagination, (2) identification, and (3) social interaction. Teaching—and education—can never be successful in the absence of any of these three key factors. Teaching—and education—depends upon relationships among *people*.

TEACHING

Natural teachers are individuals with whom learners can identify. Such teachers aren't necessarily found in schools. They are the people we would like to be like, in some ways at least, and who help and encourage us to be like them. They range from the influential if not always (to us) desirable friends that our children make in and out of school to the formal and informal associations of people that we affiliate ourselves with throughout our lives.

Effective teachers in schools and all other educational institutions are those who bring their students into contact with individuals with whom the students can most profitably and productively identify. Such teachers fulfill the three essential roles I have outlined—fostering the imagination, facilitating personal identification, and promoting social interaction. In short, effective teachers create the possibilities for experience that make worthwhile human learning possible. They bring people together in ways that permit affiliation and bonding. Technology can't do this. Identification with a computer is a pathological condition.

Teachers—human teachers, not technological ones—are crucial in educational institutions because students must have *people* they can relate to if their identities are to be strengthened and expanded in productive learning situations. Teachers spur the imagination. They are the irreplaceable essence of formal education.

In business, the "bottom line" is inevitably profit. But in education, the bottom line should always be people. A plaque on the desk of President Clinton was supposed to remind him, "It's the economy, stupid!" A constant reminder to individuals at all levels of education might be, "It's people, stupid!"

LITERACY

The assertion that people and their personal relationships are at the heart of learning often raises concern for students whose access to others is limited. What about those who can never hope to keep the company of artists, athletes, mathematicians, builders, designers, environmentalists, adventurers, and entrepreneurs, who have little access to exemplary parents, good citizens, political activists, and other role models? How will they learn what these individuals might teach them?

There is one potent way in which every community and every actual or idealized person can be made accessible to everyone, no matter how poor, shy, or physically isolated. That way is through reading. Reading is the greatest technology ever devised for bringing people together. Language is an extension of the central nervous system, and written language is the route through which the human mind can be extended into infinite realms of possibility.

A reader can identify with any character in any book, story, or article, whether "real" or fictitious (all characters are real in the reader's mind). No one can come between a reader and the character being read about. No one can say that a reader is not worthy of that character's company, or can't aspire to be like that character. Many people lead richly rewarding and often unsuspected second lives through their reading. Many have become what they are—sailors, surgeons, teachers, legislators—through inspirations and models whose acquaintance they made while reading. Reading is a uniquely powerful, private, and subversive activity.

Writing provides the additional power to create our own characters, express our feelings and develop our ideas, and submit them to our own private inspection. Long before any piece of writing influences a reader—if it ever gets that far—it symbiotically affects the person who writes it.

Of course, there are other technologies apart from reading through which we can encounter people, identify with them, and share their ideas and their feelings. We can do so through television, movies, videos, electronic games, and the Internet. But the terms of engagement are different.

The first major difference between literacy and electronic technology is in the degree of control. The authority of readers is immense. They can skip a passage, or reread it many times, just when they want, in the way they want. They can move with ease forward and backward through text and time. They can read fast or slowly. They can savor the harmony of individual words and the cadences of phrases, or ingest great gulps of meaning. They can reflect on arguments, compare alternative points of view, agree or disagree, and make mental and marginal notes in their own time. Film and television do not offer the same possibilities of self-directed involvement. It's true that computers are becoming as flexible and convenient as a book—but then the computer will *be* a book.

Writers have similar authority. They can express themselves, seize a moment of inspiration or agonize until one comes, reflect upon what they have created, test ideas on themselves and others, modify, expand, condense, interweave, and overcome time itself as they move forward or backward through the text. Little of this can be done with film, certainly with nothing like the same facility.

Fast-forwarding on a screen is not the same as skipping paragraphs or pages; slowing the action or freeze-framing is not the same as focusing on particular parts of a text; and watching or hearing images of a dispute is not the same as participating in an argument. I'm not denying the emotional and even intellectual power of electronic technologies, nor their possibility of dramatic appeal and ability to stimulate the imagination, but they could never take the place of reading and print. They are different modes of experience, not substitutes. In fact, if film and video had been invented before anyone had thought of reading and writing, it would still have been necessary, and inevitable, for reading and writing to be developed.

The second major difference between written language and electronic technologies lies in the degree of personal involvement they encompass. Reading, like language in general, is primarily an internal technology; it can never be a passive activity. Reading fires the imagination and commands identification because of the participation it demands from the reader. A reader gripped by a narrative is also controlled by the narrative—another instance of reciprocal control. A story or report that holds our attention requires a contribution on the part of the reader—in terms of background knowledge, prediction, understanding of genre, scene setting, disambiguation, gap filling, and continuity—comparable with the contribution of the author (Smith 1994). This is the reason our attention can be held by badly written novels with cardboard characters, ludicrous scenarios, and flimsy motivations; good readers flatter poor writers.

And finally, we also learn. Reading teaches itself; or rather the authors of what you read become the teachers of what they write. But we not only learn to read through reading, we can also—if we engage in an appropriate act of identification with the author—learn about writing, spelling, grammar, expression, comprehension, and reasoning. Only through reading can we practice critical thinking, experiencing how to follow and even refute a closely reasoned argument, to go beyond the sound bite. When we identify with authors and with characters in books, we can arm ourselves for many challenging aspects of life.

Hardly any of this can be accomplished with electronic technology, even that which appears to involve reading and writing, because the technology obscures the person and blocks the interpersonal relationship. Education is people, stupid! Electronic technology is heartless, mindless, and impersonal.

TECHNOLOGY AND EDUCATION

Electronic technology seems capable of extending all human capacities. It enables us to travel faster and further, extends our reach and our vision, permits us to make more complex calculations, to exchange information and ideas, and to organize vast quantities of knowledge. It helps builders to build, musicians to compose, and writers to write (it has been a boon to my professional life). I'm by no means against technology, in daily life or in the classroom. But electronic technology also helps anyone who so desires to control other people and to engage in all manner of oppressive and manipulative activities.

Technology is double edged. The equipment that helps students achieve computer literacy, whatever that might be, may also make them susceptible to mindless "teacher-proof" instruction. The computer that helps students engage in music, art, and writing can also be a teaching machine with the educational value of an arcade game. The Internet opens up worlds of information, illustration, and interaction, but it can also allow perverse tentacles of the outside world to establish themselves in classrooms.

The computer is ubiquitous, useful, and seductive. It naturally and properly appeals to many teachers, students, and other creative people. But it is also irresistible to anyone dedicated to management systems, accountability, and the economic bottom line. To such people, computers are cheaper, more efficient, and more reliable than human beings. Their efficiency resides not only in their fabled memories and speed of operation, but in their ability to organize anything that can be reduced to *data*. They are unparalleled in the establishment of records through questions, interrogations, censuses, information sharing, and (particularly in the case of reading education) tests.

Electronic technology is the inevitable next step in the systematization of education that began in the 1850s with the segregation of students on the basis of age and ability, facilitating instruction on a production line model, and creating artificial competition and bogus success and failure (Smith 1986, 1998). Mandated curriculums and the constant surveillance of teachers through test results would be impossible without computers. Computers can also administer and monitor instruction, fragmented into data-sized scraps. For anyone who believes that learning is a matter of systematic memorization, drills, exercises, tests, effort, reward, and punishment, technology is more desirable than teachers in the classroom.

Common sense might say that computers can never replace human teachers, or books—but common sense is not a consideration in most political and administrative decisions. Common sense is often seen as unreliable, emotional, and subjective. Proponents of direct instruction are notoriously mistrustful of common sense, which they denigrate as "handwaving" or "folk psychology." They prefer "scientific evidence," no matter how contrived. The allure of computers lies precisely in their total lack of emotion and subjectivity. A compassionate computer is an oxymoron.

Teachers are the most expensive line items in any educational budget. And there is no shortage of claims that commercial instructional procedures can take the place of teachers, and no shortage of politicians and editorial writers who succumb to such blandishments. And if teachers are found to be redundant in education, can school buildings be far behind? Instruction can be delivered wherever there is a television set.

Computers can't take over the teacher's role, because computers aren't human and have no feelings or sensitivity. Electronic technology can't take the place of books, because it doesn't facilitate the imaginative flow and personal identification involved in reading. None of these arguments, however, has any effect on people who believe the bottom line is economics, and that learning is simply a matter of "accessing information."

And short of a revolution, which I think is unlikely to occur and even less likely to succeed, such attitudes won't change.

After all, labor costs are a primary challenge to management experts. People are displaced where once they were essential. All around us we see the growth of tellerless banking, shopless shopping, driverless transportation, pilotless flight, and surgeonless surgery. Why should teacherless teaching be far behind?

Saying that education *needs* teachers won't protect them. People once argued that horses were essential for road and rail transport. We already hear that schools can't afford the teachers they have, that class sizes must grow, and that "interactive" technology can deliver personalized instruction.

Teachers are under pressure from all levels of government, from academics and self-proclaimed experts, and from vast commercial enterprises in the "communications" industry. Sometimes these groups work together, as they currently do in the passage of federal and state legislation mandating mindless ways in which teachers should teach reading and other subjects. But often their machinations are unobtrusive and insidious, ranging from the lobbying of legislators to purchasing influence in schools through "gifts" of programs and equipment, with guarantees of "results."

Can electronic technology take the place of teachers and books? Never. Will electronic technology take the place of teachers and books? I'm not sure.

WHO'S PRIVILEGED?

It's not difficult to see in the media who is privileged in education. Teachers are rarely in the news without being portrayed as old-fashioned, disruptive, pampered, expensive, lazy, and incompetent. Books (and music and art), if mentioned at all in the context of education, are regarded as costly frills. But it's rare to find a word of criticism toward technology.

Consider the following omens:

- Computer systems and software are widely advertised as *guaranteeing* success in learning, and even excellence, while claiming to reduce or eliminate dependence upon teachers.

See the advertisements in any popular journal dedicated to reading, education, parenting, or childhood.

• Commercial programs, often abetted by academic "consultants," offer complete curriculums to help students "reach their potential." One company, far from unique, offers four thousand hours of K–12 "interactive" curriculum with a "full set of built-in management tools."

• "Distance learning networks" are proliferating, linking thousands of educational institutions.

• Many colleges require students, who are already losing touch with their professors, to have portable computers for coursework.

• Schools, and even kindergartens, give their students computers to take home. Some schools provide computers for parents as well.

• Many parents believe their children need computers at home to "keep up" with their schoolwork.

• There is a growing use and promotion of computers for special education and for "tutorials"—a word that is rapidly changing in meaning from "meeting with a person" to "intensive instruction."

• More untrained personnel are employed in many classrooms. They are cheaper and less concerned about delegating teaching responsibilities to electronic technology.

Many articles in professional educational journals present technology in a more favorable light than teachers, incidentally or specifically. Quinlan (1997) notes that a typical Web page for an online high school composition course lists the objectives and table of contents of the course, identifies specific activities for the student *and the instructor*, and allows teachers to enrich the curriculum with resources that match the needs of their students. One wonders how composition teachers managed before.

Van Horn (1998) promises that school and university courseware in the future will contain "intelligent 'agents' that monitor, coach, and assess student performance." The need for "a few face-to-face meetings" will be handled by such "groupware" as "e-mail, conferencing, discussion groups, news groups, and desktop videoconferencing software . . . used in a moderated or unmoderated fashion to provide a variety of opportunities for synchronous and time-shifted personal interaction" (p. 556).

Diana Oblinger (1997), an IBM academic programs manager, shares a paradoxical technocratic perception that human teaching is mechanical, asserting that "the on-campus student who desires a more individualized, self-paced, self-directed learning experience can achieve that through technology" (pp. 31, 32). She then asks, "Why not allow the delivery channel [for higher education] to be managed by an organization whose core expertise is delivery?" (p. 33) noting that more colleges and universities are entering into partnerships with business that allow for such a division of labor. "Instructional software . . . has a huge potential market—and profit. Remedial education, continuing education or life-long learning and recreational learning all represent educational markets . . . that likely will be filled by commercial niche players" (p. 34). As an example she discusses how students needing remedial math could be instructed and certified by software, to remove a "costly burden" from many of our institutions.

These educational "experts" are not excluding reading instruction from their dramatic claims; in fact, reading is a lucrative target for any software company.

THE ULTIMATE COLD WAR

It is unrealistic to believe that electronic technology can be kept under control in education, much less driven out. In many ways, technology should be embraced. But in other ways, technology threatens teaching, literacy, and the arts—the fundamental sources of our growth as human beings. And there may be little that teachers, or anyone else, can do directly to delay the mindless inrush of technology into their lives. But that doesn't mean that teachers are helpless.

The "cold war" between the United States and the Soviet Union was a period of more than forty uninterrupted years of mutual hostility, fear, and bloodless conflict. The divisions between the two sides were immense and their military power enormous, yet neither was able to overthrow the other in a frontal assault. There was no winner or loser in this extended struggle, which might have continued indefinitely but for the unexpected implosion and collapse of one side.

Throughout the long standoff, two irreconcilable systems lived parallel existences, striving to assert and preserve their own values and way of life while constantly trying to undermine the power and influence of the other. There were no alliances, no compromises, just constant suspicion and watchful coexistence.

The standoff between people and technology may be a similar struggle in which neither side is able totally to prevail, but neither has to surrender. We can live alongside the encroaching technology in a new cold war, conspicuously upholding our own values, using technology where it's to our advantage, ever watchful of how it is used against us, protecting teachers and literacy.

The struggle in education is no different from that which must be fought in many aspects of national economies. We are constantly told that we can't afford the money that is spent, or should be spent, on health care, welfare, day care, working conditions, public safety, consumer protection, preserving the environment, and much else that is significant in our lives. We are barraged with the idea that any public good that does not meet the economic bottom line is unsustainable. We must always remember, and assert, that our bottom line is people.

The first step is to know the enemy, to recognize that "efficiencies" supposed to benefit the victim are in fact methodologies of constraint and control. Direct instruction is not a benevolent society. The second step is to raise awareness, in ourselves and others, of the cold war in which we are engaged. As one leading champion of literacy has declared, the primary act of literacy must be for teachers, students, and parents to examine critically the mass of official documents and academic prose that claim to be advancing literacy (Meek 1997). Who is writing the orders, planning the instruction, and setting the standards? What are their values and agendas?

The third step must be to display and proclaim our own values, to our opponents whenever possible, but constantly to our essential allies—other teachers, our students, their parents, and the public in general. Collaboration with those who want to regulate, standardize, monitor, and depersonalize should only be done under protest. Acts of defiance—insisting that people must have priority over technology—should be overt where possible and subversive where necessary. Mutual support must be the lifeblood of the teaching profession.

We can't stop technology—but this is not a message of hopelessness. We can't change the climate, but we can take advantage of the weather when it favors us and protect ourselves when it doesn't. Many classrooms are secure enclaves of imagination, identification, and personal relationships despite the storms that rage around; the irreplaceable coexisting with the irresistible.

The idea must not die that we live in a world of people, not a world of machines, systems, or lean budgets. The human heart of education must be kept beating no matter how heartless the environment in which we live, teach, and learn.

REFERENCES

Adams, Marilyn Jager. 1990. *Beginning to Read: Learning and Thinking About Print.* Cambridge, MA: MIT Press.

Allington, Richard L., ed. 2002. *Big Brother and the National Reading Curriculum: How Ideology Trumped Evidence.* Portsmouth, NH: Heinemann.

Anderson, Richard C., Elfrieda H. Hiebert, Judith A. Scott, and Ian A. G. Wilkinson. 1985. *Becoming a Nation of Readers: The Report of the Commission on Reading.* Washington, D.C.: National Academy of Education.

Barthelme, Donald. 1968. *Unspeakable Practices, Unnatural Acts.* New York: Farrar, Straus & Giroux.

Carpenter, Thomas P., Elizabeth Fennema, Megan Loef Franke, Linda Levi, and Susan B. Empson, eds. 1999. *Children's Mathematics: Cognitively Guided Instruction.* Portsmouth, NH: Heinemann.

Chall, Jeanne S. 1967. *Learning to Read: The Great Debate.* New York: McGraw-Hill.

———. 1992/1993. "Research Supports Direct Instruction Models." In "Point/Counterpoint: Whole Language Versus Direct Instruction Models." *Reading Today,* 10 (3): 8–10.

Cobb, Paul, and Heinrich Bauersfeld, eds., 1995. *The Emergence of Mathematical Meaning: Interaction in Classroom Cultures.* Hillsdale, NJ: Erlbaum.

Cohen, Jonathan D., and Jonathan W. Schooler, eds. 1997. *Scientific Approaches to Consciousness.* Mahwah, NJ: Erlbaum.

Coles, Gerald. 2000. *Misreading Reading: The Bad Science That Hurts Children*. Portsmouth, NH: Heinemann.

———. 2003. *Reading the Naked Truth: Literacy, Legislation, and Lies*. Portsmouth, NH: Heinemann.

Downing, John, and Che Kan Leong. 1982. *Psychology of Reading*. New York: Macmillan.

Downing, John, and Peter Oliver. 1973–74. "The child's conception of 'a Word.'" *Reading Research Quarterly*, 4 (9/4): 568–582.

Elley, Warwick B. 1996. "Raising Literacy Levels in Third World Countries: A Method That Works." Paper presented at the World Conference on Literacy, Philadelphia, March 1996.

Elley, Warwick, and Frances Mangubhai. 1983. "The Impact of Reading on Second Language Learning." *Reading Research Quarterly*, 19(I): 53–67.

Feynman, Richard P. 1985. *Surely You're Joking, Mr. Feynman!* Reprint, 1997. New York: Norton.

Fosnot, Catherine Twomey, ed. 1995. *Constructivism: Theory, Perspective and Practice*. New York: Teachers College Press.

Garan, Elaine M. 2002. *Resisting Reading Mandates: How to Triumph With the Truth*. Portsmouth, NH: Heinemann.

Goodman, Kenneth S. 1998a. *In Defense of Good Teaching: What Teachers Need to Know About the "Reading Wars."* York, ME: Stenhouse.

———. 1998b. Online. "Comments on the Reading Excellence Act (U.S.) (HR 2614, Senate-passed Version)." *Reading Online*, <http://www.readingonline.org/past/past_index.asp?HREF-/critical/ACT.html>. Accessed December 1998.

Kamii, Constance. 1985, 2d ed. 2000. *Young Children Reinvent Arithmetic: Implications of Piaget's Theory*. New York: Teachers College Press.

———. 1989. *Young Children Continue to Reinvent Arithmetic, 2nd Grade: Implications of Piaget's Theory*. New York: Teachers College Press.

———. 1994. *Young Children Continue to Reinvent Arithmetic, 3rd Grade: Implications of Piaget's Theory*. New York: Teachers College Press.

Kamii, Constance, and Ann Dominick. 1998. "The Harmful Effects of Algorithms in Grades 1–4," in *The Teaching and Learning of Algorithms in School Mathematics, 1998 Yearbook*, Lorna J. Morrow and Margaret J. Kenney, eds. Reston, VA: National Council of Teachers of Mathematics.

Krashen, Stephen D. 1993. *The Power of Reading: Insights from the Research*. Englewood, CO: Libraries Unlimited.

Larson, Joanne, ed. 2001. *Literacy as Snake Oil: Beyond the Quick Fix*. New York: Lang.

McNeill, Daniel. 1998. *The Face: A Natural History*. Boston, MA: Little, Brown.

Meek, Margaret. 1988. "How Texts Teach What Readers Learn." In *The Word for Teaching Is Learning: Essays for James Britton*, Martin Lightfoot and Nancy Martin, eds., London: Heinemann Educational Books.

———. 1997. "Rhetorics About Reading: Becoming Crystal Clear." *Changing English*, 4: 259–276.

Metcalf, Stephen. 2002. "Reading Between the Lines." *The Nation*, 28 January.

National Council of Teachers of English. 2002. "NCTE Members Urge Congress to Review Reading First Initiative." *The Council Chronicle*, 12 (3): 1, 4–5.

National Reading Panel. 2000. *Teaching Children to Read: An Evidence-Based Assessment of the Scientific Research Literature on Reading and Its Implications for Reading Instruction*. Washington, D.C.: National Institute of Child Health and Human Development.

Oblinger, Diana G. 1997. "High Tech Takes the High Road: New Players in Higher Education," *Educational Record*, 78: 30–34.

Paterson, Frances A. 2002. "The Politics of Phonics." *Journal of Curriculum and Supervision*, 15 (3). Reprinted in Allington (2002).

Quinlan, Laurie R. 1997. "The Digital Classroom." *TechTrends for Leaders in Education and Training*, 42: 6–9.

Saxe, Geoffrey B. 1991. *Culture and Cognitive Development: Studies in Mathematical Understanding*. Hillsdale, NJ: Erlbaum.

Smith, Frank. 1986. *Insult to Intelligence: The Bureaucratic Invasion of Our Classrooms*. Portsmouth, NH: Heinemann.

———. 1988. *Joining the Literacy Club*. Portsmouth, NH: Heinemann.

———. 1994. *Understanding Reading* (5th ed.). Hillsdale, NJ: Erlbaum.

———. 1997. *Reading Without Nonsense* (3d ed.). New York: Teachers College Press.

———. 1998. *The Book of Learning and Forgetting*. New York: Teachers College Press.

———. 1999a. "When Irresistible Technology Meets Irreplaceable Teachers." *Language Arts*, 76 (2): 414–421.

———. 1999b. "Why Systematic Phonics and Phonemic Awareness Instruction Constitute an Educational Hazard." *Language Arts*, 77 (2): 414–421.

———. 2001. "Just a Matter of Time." *Phi Delta Kappan*, 82 (8): 572–576.

———. 2002. *The Glass Wall: Why Mathematics Can Seem Difficult*. New York: Teachers College Press.

———. 2003. "The Just So Story—Obvious but False." *Language Arts*, 80 (4): 10–12.

Snow, Catherine E., M. Susan Burns, and Peg Griffin. 1998. *Preventing Reading Difficulties in Young Children*. Washington, D.C.: National Academy Press.

Taylor, Denny. 1999. "Beginning to Read and the Spin Doctors of Science: An Excerpt." *Language Arts*, 76 (3): 217–231.

Trelease, Jim, and Stephen D. Krashen. 1996. "Eating and Reading in the Library." *Emergency Librarian*, 2 (5): 27.

Van Horn, Royal. 1998. "Tomorrow's High-performance Courseware: A Rough Sketch." *Phi Delta Kappan*, 79: 556–558.

Weintraub, Sam. 1986. "The Fuzzy Area of Literature Reviews." In *Summary of Investigations Relating to Reading: July 1, 1984 to June 30, 1985*. Sam Weintraub, Helen K. Smith, Nancy L. Roser, Walter J. Moore, Michael W. Kibby, Kathleen S. Jongsma, and Peter L. Fisher, eds. Newark, DE: International Reading Association.

Yatvin, Joanne. 2002. "Babes in the Woods: The Wanderings of the National Reading Panel." *Phi Delta Kappan*, 83 (5): 364–369. Reprinted in Allington (2002).

AUTHOR INDEX

SUBJECT INDEX

ABOUT THE AUTHOR

Frank Smith has always been fascinated by language. He worked as a journalist in many countries before beginning formal academic studies in Australia. This led to a Ph.D. at Harvard University and further world travel researching, lecturing and writing. He has been a professor at the Ontario Institute for Studies in Education, the University of Toronto, the University of Victoria, British Columbia, and the University of Witswatersrand, South Africa. He has published many books and articles on human thought and learning, and lives (when he is at home) on Vancouver Island, Canada.